H.O.M.E.

Strategies for making
home a SUCCESS
during and after
treatment

HILARY MOSES, MSW
JEN MURPHY, M.Ed.

H.O.M.E. Publishing © 2023

H.O.M.E.: Strategies for Making Home a SUCCESS During and After Treatment.

Cover Design by Stephen Ambagis

ISBNs:
979-8-9874861-0-8
979-8-9874861-1-5

Disclaimer: While this book is about mental health and wellness for parents and their children, it should not be used as a substitute for seeking treatment and personalized advice from a professional credentialed in the mental health field.

Published by:

Dedication

To parents and kids who are working to make home a success for themselves and who have taught us so much along the way.

Acknowledgments

To each other for continuing to support and inspire each other while writing this book and for the ongoing push to be better versions of ourselves both professionally and personally.

To the Solutions Parenting Support team for being a group of inspiring and amazing humans that continue to challenge, fulfill, and encourage us. Thank you for being a team we love to learn and laugh with.

To colleagues throughout our careers—there are too many of you to name. You know who you are, and we are endlessly grateful for the support you have given in our personal and professional growth throughout the years.

To family and friends who have supported us through the ups and downs in our own journeys. It is only with your support that we can take the leap of faith in a project like this because we know we have a safe place to land.

To our beta readers, without you this book would not be what it is. Thank you for your willingness and your wisdom.

To Burning Soul Press for the guidance, structure, prodding, and encouragement that having our voices heard could truly affect the lives of many.

Authors' Note

Our book, H.O.M.E., is meant as a companion to walk alongside you as you embark on this journey with your family and as you support a child in wilderness therapy and beyond. It is not meant as a replacement for professional help or as an all-seeing, all-knowing guide for what your family needs. You know your family's uniqueness and our hope is that you, with the help of the team around you, can implement our insights and tips in ways that consider the emotional, mental, behavioral, or spiritual challenge your child or your family might be facing.

Throughout H.O.M.E., we share snippets of stories from the parents we have supported over time, both in our careers as wilderness therapists and as parent coaches. These stories, meant to help you solidify the learning and remember that you are not alone, are not fictional but are shaped to protect identity and names have been changed.

In order to prioritize gender inclusivity, throughout H.O.M.E., we alternate between the pronouns he, she, they.

Contents

Introduction

When we decided to write a book together, we asked ourselves two questions: who do we want to write for and why? Our answers and the passion behind them are very similar, which inspired us to press forward while keeping our reader in mind every time we sat down to write: the individual parents we have supported over the last 20 years, the parents who fight tirelessly for the emotional stability of their children and families, and the parents we have made strong connections with, shared our guidance with, and to whom we are grateful for allowing us to be a part of their moments of growth and success.

We both earned our master's degrees, went through years of supervision and training, and became licensed clinicians. Jen has a Master of Education, and is a licensed professional counselor and Hilary has a Master of Social Work and is a licensed clinical social worker. We have lived very parallel lives in our extensive wilderness therapy careers, and both have been sought out therapists who pioneered many of the successful therapeutic approaches still used today.

Hilary started her career with a summer in wilderness therapy as a field staff, supporting and guiding students in the daily therapeutic experiences. She went on to finish her master's degree and, having been so moved by her time in the wilderness therapy environment, witnessing growth she had not seen in any traditional setting, she chose to use her clinical training as a wilderness therapist. While providing direct clinical support for 15 years as a wilderness therapist, Hilary also served as the clinical director of two highly acclaimed wilderness programs, including heading the development and implementation of the family therapy program.

INTRODUCTION

Jen earned her master's and completed post-graduate studies in Advanced Diagnostics and Assessments. After exhausting the possibilities of experiential therapies that living in the Midwest offered, Jen headed west to seek out a position as a wilderness therapist, spending the next 10 years with two highly regarded wilderness programs as a therapist and assistant clinical director. In 2010, Jen decided that she wanted to spend more time directly supporting parents, providing the tools to sustain all the work their children had done in wilderness therapy. She developed and implemented a successful, nationally recognized transition program for the wilderness program she was with and ultimately created her own program, Solutions Transition Support.

Our paths finally crossed while both supporting several shared families, offering us the opportunity to collaborate and to easily align with what Hilary had espoused for years: that we were not doing enough to shape home life with parents. Hilary believed that, with more intention and focus on the parents, more kids might be able to go home from treatment sooner and with more success. It was readily apparent that Hilary and Jen were meant to contribute their passion and skills hand-in-hand, leading us to co-found Solutions Parenting Support.

During the creation of Solutions Parenting Support, we determined the purpose would be to help parents trust themselves again. We want to help parents be honest with themselves as they explore their own strengths and struggles, and help them better understand how to keep their kids' strengths and struggles in mind as they shape the expectations and tone of their home. We want to encourage parents to understand the importance of their own boundaries, the importance of knowing what they have control over and the importance of redefining the outcomes they are aiming for.

H.O.M.E.

Our goal is to teach, guide, and provide resources that we believe are effective and then allow parents to integrate them as their own so they can authentically reap the benefits. We will forever sing it from the rooftops that parenting and co-parenting are the most difficult jobs out there and we have fumbled and stumbled ourselves as parents even while wearing the hats of parenting experts. If we were starting a movement with this book, it would be to get more kids home from treatment sooner, increase the sustainability of the amazing work that is done in treatment, and help parents see how important their role is throughout.

We wrote this book for you, the parent who has spent day in and day out for months fighting for your child's stability, trying everything you know and testing out every piece of professional advice you were given. This is for you who, after all of that, had to make the decision to remove your child from your home to get him more help than he would allow you to give him. We are writing to you, the parent, who invested in the program as much as you could but the reality is you were only able to do so much of your own work while he was away. We are writing to you, the parent who is completely over-whelmed by financial fear and doubling down at work as you have immense responsibilities, all while trying to recover from the experiences that led you to sending your child to treatment. We are writing this for you, the parent who now has a child coming home from treatment, unclear about how authentic his gains are or how he is going to show up and what will be different.

We are writing to you, the parent whose anxiety is high as you watch your 20-year-old flailing in college or your young adult child grappling with a myriad of obstacles, such as substance abuse and social anxiety, and stuck as a "parent-funded" young adult. To the parent who had an "unparentable" child when she was home, refusing to follow rules, becoming

3

verbally aggressive and sometimes physically aggressive when you tried to establish healthy boundaries and keep her on the right track. You ended up focusing on the things she was doing wrong because it was challenging to find things she was doing well. And now, being unclear about what she has gained through treatment, it is time to try again.

You are hoping that she has new insight and maturity and that, even if you don't have the full understanding of her strengths and struggles, you hope she will have learned something to manage her internal world in healthier ways. And you are scared. You are worried that things will go back to what they used to be, scared that you cannot be enough of what she needs, worried that she has not learned enough, fearful that the school system cannot support kids like her, worried that you will have spent way more money than you can afford, and your uncertainties can feel crippling.

And to some extent, you are right. Being enough is something we all want to achieve, though the reality is, you are not enough, he did not learn enough, the school system cannot support enough, and you spent a ton of money, time, energy, and emotion in hopes of a "fix" so grand that it is not possible. He is still him. He still struggles. And you are still here, in this situation, with a child you love with everything you have, even in the times when he is hard to like; he is who he is, and you are who you are, and you have to find a path through.

This book is for you to lean on in times of uncertainty. This book can be a partner to brainstorm with that knows deeply the situation you are in. This book understands why you attend less and less social events, because at times you're not only exhausted, but you have to wear a façade while everyone talks about how their kids are doing. The last thing you want to do is be asked about your kids or talk about the hot mess that has been your life the last few years. As they talk about the sports teams their kids are on or the colleges they are looking at, you sit there, hopeful that you won't be noticed so no one asks you how your kids are. You don't want the shame, or the pity, or the unknowing stares, or cooing pep talks. You just don't want any of it, except maybe the wine or margarita but, since you are trying to stay sober to support your son who was caught taking your alcohol before trying to run off in the middle of the night, even the healthy social enjoyment of drinking is out of the question.

We wrote this book for you, to share the tools that have staying power for parents who are making changes or sustaining changes when bringing their child home from treatment. This book is not a magic wand, nor does it have all the secret passwords or know all the hidden tunnels. It can make you laugh at times and maybe cry at others, but it can also be a reminder there are some things you do have control over. You can change the tone of your household, you can role model that being an adult can be pretty amazing, you can discover tips for regulating yourself, even simultaneously as your child dysregulates, so that when you decide to intervene or redirect the situation, you can do it from a place of balance, of increased internal calm and with a wise-minded approach. This book is here to help you walk away from challenging parenting moments feeling great about how you showed up, even if your child's behavior did not change.

Often, we get the privilege to connect with former wilderness therapy clients. One client we met a decade later at a conference, which he was attending because he was then working in a recovery-based treatment program. We asked him if he could share lessons for parents we were currently supporting as parenting coaches – things that he would want parents going through this process to know. He shared his story of going home after 15 months in treatment to parents who were still feeling their own guilt, embarrassment, and shame about having sent their child to treatment. They had not enlisted any support in their community due to these deep feelings, assuming no one around them was struggling in the same ways, and no one would understand their decision to send their child away to treatment.

"I was too immature at the time to keep it all going," he said. "I had no peer support, and my parents were walking on eggshells, hesitant to disappoint me as I exploited their guilt." He went on to say that he needed his parents to feel confident in their decision and he needed them to outwait him.

"I needed them to not give up on me and to not see my challenges in an 'all is lost' sort of way." At times, he said, they made comments to the effect that treatment was a waste of time and money as they saw him start to struggle again, which led them to feel even more guilty and resentful about the process. As they lost hope and ran the narrative that treatment was for nothing, he began to believe the same story, even though, "it was truly life changing for me and I needed them to believe it was helpful even in the moments they could not see it."

We wrote this book and share this story for you, the parent, who needs the support to find resources and the guidance to implement tools that will help your child sustain all the work you have asked him to invest in. We wrote this book to remind you that, by intervening in his world and sending him to treatment, you took a stand to encourage him to help himself and made a commitment to do the same for yourself.

You will find "Nuggets of Knowledge" and exercises throughout, which we invite you to explore in ways that fit for you, your values, and your uniqueness. There is no right or wrong way to approach the exercises and your job, in part, is to identify what challenges and encourages you along the way. You will also find summaries entitled, "Remember, Reflect, Revisit" which are meant to solidify your learning.

The H.O.M.E. Model

We resisted developing a model for years, mainly to protect the individuality of each family we supported as well as the uniqueness of our coaches, with their personalities, experience, and expertise. We did not want to put anyone in a box by pushing people through a model that might not be a fit. However, after supporting hundreds of families, we started to witness patterns and similarities, which compelled us to codify them to meet our mission to make home be a success during and after treatment.

We realized that each of our distinct coaching approaches walked parents back and forth along the H.O.M.E. continuum, which empowers parents to sustain their personal growth through situational self-assessment. In our work, parents present us with a situation. Together we assess their capabilities, their strengths and struggles and start to understand the makeup of their child and family. Additionally, we created a model that offers parents specific questions for self-reflection and self-assessment and to present them with empowering language to guide themselves as they learn and put new skills into practice.

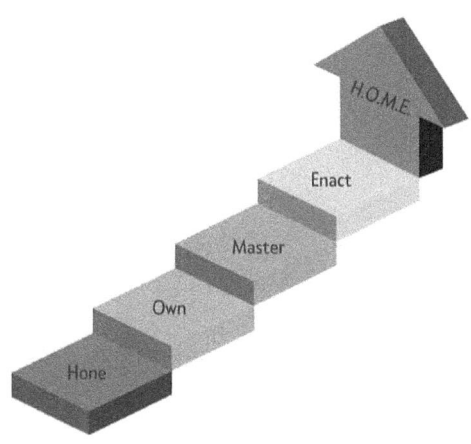

Hone. When you **hone**, you sharpen your understanding of the situation in front of you and what is underlying it, both for you and for others involved; you get clear on the skills you need to learn through a process of data collection and collaboration; you learn the foundations of new communication, relationship, and parenting skills; your home contract takes shape and you learn to set and communicate goals and expectations clearly.

Own. Ownership is key to knowing what you have control over. Knowing what you have control over empowers you to focus your energy where it matters most. In this step, you develop a clearer understanding of these skills you want to **hone**, you confront the challenges in front of you and you gain a better understanding of the need for change and evolution in your relationships and parenting skills.

Master. Just as you hope that your child develops **mastery** over the tools they learn in treatment, we encourage you to practice the skills you are being taught and gain a greater clarity and confidence in understanding why they work.

Enact. As you **own** and **master** these skills, your next step is to put these new skills into action regularly and with clarity and confidence. As you assess situations after the fact, you can ask yourself if you did or did not **enact** the skills that you have. When you are able to **enact**, to take action on things over which you have control, regardless of your child's behavior, you will take charge of the tone of your home.

The H.O.M.E. model considers the process of developing new habits as being on a continuum, thus we recognize the H.O.M.E. model is not always a linear process. It is important that parents use the continuum to assess a situation for themselves. To better understand the continuum and how to identify where you are and what you need, get comfortable asking yourself questions like: Where am I with this specific situation? Do I have a skill I need to **hone**? Is there something I need to **own** that I have not yet? Have I **mastered** a tool that I simply need to remember to **enact**? Or am I **enacting** my skills and am I in a good rhythm of interactions and responses?

Throughout this book, we share stories about parents who have self-assessed where they land on the continuum to help guide themselves thoughtfully forward. We further incorporate questions and suggestions to illustrate how you can put this continuum into action for yourselves.

We understand change is a continuum and that you will move through this model at different paces in relation to different skills and parenting styles and struggles. Just as a homing device finds a path through, using the H.O.M.E. model again and again helps you to define and refine what is needed to **hone** in on the path the family system needs to take to find more and continued success.

The Elephant in the Room

The Breaking Code Silence movement is one of several avenues through which the safety and efficacy of wilderness therapy and residential treatment programs have been scrutinized. Former clients and/or their parents are sharing their challenging experiences and some report feeling traumatized by the experience they had in treatment.

We have witnessed several factors that contribute to negative experiences for a child or family: the severity of mental health challenges in the child and family, unsafe behaviors such as self-harm that led to physical holds to keep children from hurting themselves and others, the developmental stage of a program, and its staff and training, validated therapeutic treatment at the time that are not a fit for all, accidents and unknown underlying health concerns.

As with every institution in charge of caring for others (public and private schools, intensive outpatient programs, drug and alcohol treatment centers, eldercare facilities) this field should be evaluated for maintaining high standards of health and safety. It is difficult to not get defensive when we have witnessed the life-changing effects of wilderness therapy. It is hard to not point out that in any institution, not every tragedy can be avoided.

There is a spotlight on the risks with the wilderness therapy industry while people are facing the tragedies of school shootings, the high numbers of adolescent and young adult overdoses and suicides, and ongoing domestic violence and abuse in the home. We share this only for perspective, not to make excuses. There is no excuse for allowing avoidable trauma to occur. For every negative experience we have heard of in wilderness therapy, we can count at least three former students who have reached out to thank us for the role we played in turning their lives around, some even choosing to work in the field of wilderness therapy.

One parent, Martha, whose daughter went to wilderness therapy, shared how hard it could be to wade through the stories shared on the internet and concerns expressed by friends and family members, and discern what was best for their family.

"Parents entering this decision making process about wilderness therapy are going to Google it and the voices with the worst experience are the loudest and most active," Martha mentioned. The pressures parents like Martha have felt to mistrust wilderness therapy have impacted their internal narrative of their own experiences and stirred fear, though they were equally afraid of making the choice to not intervene with out-of-home support. The key for these parents was to develop a wise-minded approach, a tool which we expand upon in our guiding principles, and to advocate for information throughout the process, looking to factual information and not just the negative narrative from the internet to guide them.

When we ask former clients who had positive experiences why they tend not to voice their opinions to balance the negative perspective, they have often said something along the lines of, "I am living my life in healthy ways and have other things to spend my time on. I had a great experience, and I am thankful for it, but now thriving in my current day-to-day is my priority."

Parents in the position of choosing alternative support such as wilderness therapy for their child often are afraid of the consequences of their options: not doing anything or choosing wilderness therapy. Additionally, the opinions that friends and extended family members carry can increase the dissonance a parent experiences and can leave a parent feeling more alone, unable to find impartial support. While there is value in hearing the opinions and concerns from your family and friends, it's important to not let those narratives be the only ones that shape what you see.

We encourage you to do your due diligence, not to make decisions with fear as the guide, reach out for support as you explore your options, and have a scrutinous eye without taking only the negative stories as the full truth. Know that you are not alone.

Guiding Principles

Our guiding principles are the concepts we often tie into parent coaching, regardless of what stage a parent is in with their struggling adolescent or young adult. In our work with so many parents, these guiding principles provide reliable benefits as parents dive into understanding and utilizing them with great success. The benefits include improving self-regulation by learning to have reasonable expectations of themselves as well as their children, and feeling empowered to shape the tone of the home in ways that serve the whole family system. When parents invest in the H.O.M.E. model, self-assessing what their needs are, and can **hone**, **own**, **master**, or **enact** skills with the following guiding principles in mind, they tend to have increased capability in their parenting and report success in **mastering** what they have control over.

Our guiding principles include: starting from a place of curiosity, increasing a parent's knowledge base to understand the human growth and development stages of our children and emerging young adults, developing a wise-minded parenting gut, and noticing and claiming what you as a parent have control over. Additionally, the guiding principles of captaining your ship and buying time energize the exhausted parent.

While we have education, training, licenses, and experiences with thousands of families to inform these guiding principles, we also spend a significant amount of time educating ourselves, increasing our theoretical knowledge, and surrounding ourselves with colleagues who empower us, challenge our thinking, and share their wisdom with us, which we apply to our coaching practice. We would be lying if we didn't say that some of what we espouse is the greatness borrowed from others. Throughout this book we will tie in these guiding principles and concepts that we are hoping will encourage habit-forming changes.

Guiding Principle 1:
Engage with Curiosity

Curiosity is simply the desire to learn, and this can translate to the desire to understand others, which is why we encourage you to start your interactions from a place of curiosity. Slowing down your reaction time and using curiosity with your partner or your child can help to shape the tone of an interaction.

Have you ever been part of a conversation where you start to share a story and you are interrupted by your companion, who says some version of, "Oh, that happened to me, too, and when it did, I..." and then proceeds to take over the conversation? In part, this is how we relate as humans and the habit is not entirely unhealthy, but there are times when we want our stories, the experiences that we share, to get a bit more airtime for us to feel truly heard, seen, and valued.

"Active listening" is a common teaching in the art of communication and building healthy relationships, and you are likely to be introduced to this early on in any relationship-focused therapy or coaching. With active listening, the goal is to quiet your personal narrative, to attune your attention to the other and to make a conscious effort to truly understand and retain the information that is being shared with you. Rather than waiting for a break in the other's narrative so you can insert your story or opinion, you focus on being genuinely curious about your conversation partner's experience. The phrase, "tell me more," when used with an authentic, natural tone, is an open invitation for the speaker to keep the floor. You can show interest and true curiosity without agreeing with or condoning what is being shared. Engaging with curiosity is often our recommendation as a first step in any exchange.

If you guide yourself toward the habit of starting with curiosity, you also slow yourself down, give yourself a chance to regulate before you respond, and have a better shot at helping the other person feel truly heard. A statement such as, "I want to make sure I am getting what you are saying, tell me more," could be helpful. We encourage you to find statements that fit your personality and style and that illustrate genuine curiosity.

Guiding Principle 2:
Human Growth & Development: The Actual Instruction Manual

Generations of parents around the world have said in exhaustion, "Kids don't come with an instructional manual". We actually believe they do. That "manual" can be found within any Human Growth and Development college textbook or online resource that gives parents the knowledge of one's lifelong process of physical, behavioral, cognitive, and emotional growth and change and the typical milestones that go along with each.

From a foundational place, the study of human growth and development has evolved over time, just as we have as humans. Some awareness of human growth and development helps you to determine what we are seeing in our kids that is age-appropriate and what might be more concerning. This can also help us to **hone** responses that fit the child's developmental capabilities.

In our parent coaching, we use the evolving science of human growth to guide parents with forming reasonable expectations and distinguishing "clinically significant" behaviors from developmentally appropriate ones. What is important to note is that the life span stages and milestones are ever-changing; the rate at which the brain develops and at which specific sections of the brain develop, has slowed. You might hear about your child's struggle with "executive functioning" for example. While some children struggle more than others in this area, we are seeing delayed development in this area of the brain across the board with the families we support. These evolving insights force us to identify what we are seeing as parents, acknowledge how we are responding to their developmental changes, and to encourage us to be more strategic in our parenting.

Additionally, they allow us to identify what we can expect and what our children are capable of during these stages in life. Are we expecting too much or too little? Are they truly capable of following through with a commitment during certain developmental stages? If we understood developmental stages, would we really be so surprised at what our kids do or say?

When faced with a challenging situation, putting curiosity into action, keeping in mind human development, and using the H.O.M.E. continuum to assess your role in a situation, you can ask yourself, "is now a time that I need to **hone** my understanding of what is developmentally appropriate before I respond with shock and surprise to this situation?" Our belief is we would be much less surprised and we would be more prepared if we, as parents, committed to knowing and understanding our children as they grow and are shaped by each developmental stage.

Guiding Principle 3:
Wise-Minded Parenting Gut

Thinking or acting with a wise mind refers to the ability to approach a situation balancing the emotional and the practical – the wise-mind is the middle ground. Our passion burns for this principle: to help parents find and trust this part of themselves, whether for the first time or rediscovering it. This principle compels us in this work. A "wise-minded parenting gut" is a gut feeling or instinct that is driven by the middle ground, not leaning heavily toward an emotional response or practical response.

We, collectively as parents, need to remember the importance of behaving like the adults we hope our children grow to become. The obstacles for living true to that come in those moments when we are not regulating our emotions. Perhaps we are hyper-focused on how we think something should be or we misunderstand something because we have a presumption that is taking over our focus. Regardless, in those moments we either emotionally parent or rationally parent. Acting in wise-minded ways means we are balancing the emotional and the rational in order to consider both in our response. As parents, it is so important that we learn to trust our parenting gut, even if it is wrong sometimes and the first step toward that, in our opinion, is to understand where the voice of your parenting gut is coming from.

One of the gifts therapy or professional coaching can provide is clarity, if you are open to receiving it. These opportunities can be a mirror into which you look to better understand yourself, your past, your present, and your future and how they all are intertwined. Professional therapy and coaching can be an exploratory place where you ask yourself the hard questions that you tend to avoid in the day-to-day because, who has the time, the space, or the energy? It can be the place where you go to shed the defenses of blame in order to look at yourself, your patterns, your choices, your emotions and to claim the things you can, while **honing** your understanding of what you want to do with it all once you realize it is yours to do something with.

If, for example, you experienced some form of childhood trauma or are the adult child of an alcoholic parent, some of your decisions and reactions might come from the voice of those experiences without accounting for certain aspects of the current situation that differentiate it from your past experiences. Sometimes we are engaged in an argument with someone who is not even in the room.

As you head into this experience of supporting your child in treatment, whether you are forming opinions on how things are going or writing letters or showing up for your family at home, ask yourself what it would take to approach a situation in a wise-minded way. What might you need to **own**? What might you need to **master** or **enact** to trust that your wise mind is at the wheel?

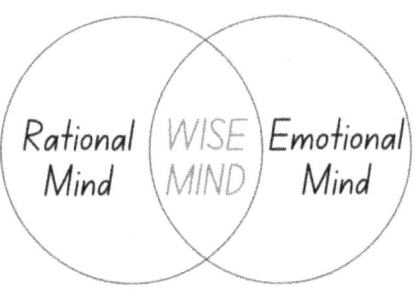

Guiding Principle 4:

What You Have Control Over

We've heard it a hundred times: we can only control ourselves and our reactions to our emotions. That doesn't mean it's easy to remember when everything feels out of control. This is one of the most challenging aspects of parenting to truly accept; we know, or we tend to believe we know, all the right moves for our kids to make. We know how to approach school, the importance of sticking to commitments, the value of a balanced life and physical activity, the importance of limiting technology and so on. When our children become pre-teens and adolescents headed toward young adulthood, we can only shine a light on the "right" path, set up guardrails, and hope our children make healthy decisions. We watch them dig deep holes with their stubbornness, and we see how they negatively contribute to their mental, emotional, and social health, complain about it, and do little to help themselves. We take the blame – a lot of the blame – often.

In the world of parent coaching, getting clear about what you do and don't have control over as a parent is key. Time, energy, and emotional currency are in limited supply; identifying areas over which you have control as well as the higher risk, more important areas over which to exert that control, can help parents to conserve energy.

To guide yourself forward in a situation using questions related to the H.O.M.E. model, ask yourself, "what about this moment do I have control over so that I can **own** it and **enact** a skill?" Your answer could include, "I can **own** my ability to self-regulate and to have boundaries that direct my choices." For example, you cannot control if your kid gets out of bed and goes to school, but you can control the role you choose to play in the morning – validating the challenges they might be experiencing, helping your teen understand the pros and cons of their decisions, offering options within which they can make choices, and putting parent-imposed consequences into place.

In the moments you wish your teen was writing in their journal, going to therapy, practicing the meditation they learned while in wilderness therapy, or getting outside to get some movement and put down their devices, you can take the first step by ensuring that you are doing each yourself, **owning** your choices and modeling as the adult you hope your child grows to become.

Similarly, we encourage exploring the question, "Am I modeling adulthood in a way that encourages my kids to want to grow to become adults?" **Own** what you have control over. Rather than solely focusing on directing children to make more responsible decisions, try also to expose them to the importance of finding joy in adulthood. In "The Book of Joy", the Dalai Lama and Sir Desmond Tutu identify aspects of joy such as contentment, pleasure, gratitude, amusement, and wonder. Let's start the revolution of joy and playfulness in adulthood because it sure seems lost at times.

We see our children holed up in their rooms and are desperate for them to experience a broader world but, are we modeling the message we want to convey? Through the COVID-19 pandemic, our children witnessed more of the day-to-day in the world of adults and we often asked families if they felt their kids were getting the experience that being an adult was desirable or if they witnessed only the stress, frustration, irritability, alcohol overuse, and tension-filled relationships. Are we showing our kids that it is worth it to make it out of childhood and adolescence? Many teens express not wanting to grow up, not being able to tolerate the responsibilities and hard work that it might take, not understanding why it is worth it, being too anxious to even learn to drive. The children of the families we support show that anxiety and depression are peaking, as are suicidal and self-harm tendencies.

As such, we invite parents to really look at themselves and at their lives to see what transformation is possible to ensure that you are enjoying your lives. Sometimes simply writing down the small and passing delights of each day, pausing for long enough to even notice that a moment was delightful. We also invite parents to examine what they have control over while practicing emotional regulation to better manage the frustration over the control we don't have. We can help you to shape the tone of your home in ways of which you can feel proud.

Guiding Principle 5:

Captain Your Ship

While we guide parents to learn to collaborate in age-appropriate ways with their children, we typically include the reminder that you are the parent. To take on the role of parenting means that you can take responsibility for leading the charge, guiding with confidence, and **owning** when you stumble through new situations.

Susan Stiffelman in "Parenting Without Power Struggles" talks about being the captain of your ship and highlights how often we give over the captain role to kids of all ages who are not quite able to consider all factors when it comes to steering and staying on course. Imagine you were on a cruise and trusting that the captain has the expertise to be in charge of keeping everyone safe and on course to the intended destination. Picture an anxious passenger expressing concern about the direction of things or an entitled one deciding they don't like the destination and want a new one. If the captain changed courses with each bit of feedback from passengers, you might lose faith in their ability to be in charge. Now, the captain might gather information from other experienced colleagues and from the crew and she might even consider feedback from the passengers as she chooses what is best for everyone but that is just it – her job is to take feedback in and use her expertise to make the final decision. Her job is not to please others and change course because someone demands it.

Within the realm of parent coaching, we help parents to earn, and remember that you have earned, the right to be at the helm. With the H.O.M.E. continuum questions in mind, you can ask, "while **mastering** my wise mind to make decisions, what skills can I **enact** to earn trust that I am the captain here?" One of your answers might be: "I need to follow through with the boundary that I set and not change it when my child is upset and negotiating."

With anything that is worth doing well, especially with parenting, it is important to stay engaged in learning and to continue to build your expertise. Constant learning allows you to guide your family through a values-based lens and with faith in your competence. To make family-focused decisions, you might hear what is going on with others and take concerns into account while recognizing that the final decision is yours. You are the captain of your ship for a reason. To support this process, we encourage parents to be very clear about the "why" behind your choice and to take the time to make thoughtful decisions. If you are anchored to your values and clear about your why, then you are less likely to be blown off course by the storm of your children.

Guiding Principle 6:

Buy Yourself Time

Buying yourself time simply suggests that not everything needs an answer right now nor does it need to be driven from the "right now" emotions that are stirred. Our kids, in our current world of instant gratification, no matter their age and especially when they want something, can make us feel as if everything is an urgent, important situation that needs to get dealt with "right now." Whether it is a last-minute request to borrow the car, to quickly and immediately change already-set plans or the need to stay on the phone 30 minutes later than what is agreed to, parents often experience the pressure of feeling trapped and put the expectation on themselves to make a quick, pressured decision. Well, you don't need to respond in kind. In fact, in order to come from a more wise-minded place that can enable you to make a decision you feel good about, buying yourself time is the number one guiding principle to **enact**.

How often do we make a decision when we are in fight or flight mode (the automatic mode from which we function in stressful events)? Often, 20 minutes after announcing our decision, once our brains are working at full capacity, we wish we hadn't. Some parents we support have talked about their children following them around the house, into the bathroom even, to get an answer right now. When we are pushed to make decisions in the moment, we are often in fight or flight mode, which in this case, is our automatic reaction to the perceived urgency of the situation – the urgency that someone else, our child, has created. When our children have a hard time hearing "no", the perceived urgency then turns into a perceived threat which activates the sympathetic nervous system and triggers an acute stress response as it's preparing the body to fight or flee.

One way to execute the principle of buying time is to utilize language that is so consistent, it becomes a mantra that you will just expect yourself to say, and your child will expect to hear it from you whenever requests need to be considered. We encourage the mantra or your version of "If you need an answer now, the answer is no, if you give me time to think about it and all that I need to consider, and you wait for me to come to you, you may get a different answer." When buying yourself time in this way, in order to earn trust that you are the captain(s) of the ship, you need to hold true to your end of the deal. Make sure you follow up with your kids when you say you will, even when it's difficult to give them an answer they may not like or agree with. Our children know that we forget, they know we avoid... that is, in part, why they follow us around until we cave and give them what they want. So, buy yourself time and be transparent with your kids about why you are doing it.

When you buy yourself time, you have a greater chance of **enacting** critical thinking, which furthers your ability to shape the tone of your home. Critical thinking is the objective analysis of an issue to form a judgment that is free from personal bias. Many families we support identify rigid thinking as an obstacle they face with their children and even with themselves. Critical thinking can enhance the ability to think flexibly and thus bolster resilience. It's important to remember that critical thinking is taught, it's not something we are necessarily born with, it's not even something that comes naturally. The more you as a parent focus on the practice of critical thinking, from the solid foundation you have as an adult, the more flexible you will become in your interactions with your child as you observe and encourage the development of their own effective reasoning skills.

Now you have a bit of a foundation and a small window into our philosophies and style. With these guiding principles in mind, we invite you to take the first next steps along the path from where you are to where you want to be as you aim to **hone**, **own**, **master** and **enact** strategies for making home a success during and after your child's experience in treatment.

Remember. Reflect. Revisit.

- Curiosity: Slow your reaction time, express true interest in others' stories, ask your version of "tell me more".
- Human Growth and Development: There are developmentally appropriate emotions/interactions/behaviors our kids illustrate and there are more clinically significant ones. Approach your kids with curiosity and ask for help to discern intent or meaning before placing judgment or emotionally reacting.

- Develop a wise-minded parenting gut: Before you let your gut direct your life, know where the voice of it is coming from so that you can build trust in it.
- Notice and **own** what you have control over: Save your emotional currency by asking, "what can I **enact** based on what I have control over in this situation?"
- Captain your ship: Using a wise-minded gut, make decisions you feel confident sticking to in order to earn your spot at the helm.
- Buy yourself time: When in doubt, slow down. Most situations are not the urgent emergency that we, or our kids, make us feel they are.

PART 1

Hone & Own:
The Treatment Journey

PART 1

Hone & Own:
The Treatment Journey

This section guides you through aspects of the treatment journey, encourages you to acknowledge the challenges you have faced and honor the important work ahead of you.

While the treatment journey can look different for different families in different situations, many families we work with start their journey in wilderness therapy. However, we touch on something for everyone to guide you along the way, no matter where you and your child's journey started or currently is in the treatment journey.

In Part 1, our focus embraces parents whose children are just beginning their treatment journey in wilderness therapy. Part 2 is for everyone, regardless of where one is in the treatment process, as it focuses on the personal work that parents can do for themselves, which can have residual effect on all familial relationships and help shape the new tone of the home. We hope parents come back to Part 2 as needed. Part 3 supports parents whose children are preparing to transition from the supportive therapeutic placements where their journeys have taken them, whether wilderness therapy or longer term residential treatment, and who are continuing their journey outside of treatment. Whether in the home or in another place where parents are the primary support, Part 3 guides reinforcement of the children as they work to build themselves up in the best ways they can.

While you have a child in treatment, we invite you to invest the time you have now in a parallel process. Your child will have reflective time to herself, will be faced with grief about this new reality, will accomplish physical tasks to reinvigorate her competency, will engage in a peer group that is challenging her to be her best self, and she will explore herself internally to better understand the driving factors beneath recent challenges. This is the time for you to explore alongside her by making the commitment and finding the time to engage in your own process.

The topics we address in this section will help you with the first two facets of the H.O.M.E. model: **hone** and **own**. While you have a child in treatment, this might include sharpening your awareness of the strengths and struggles that contributed to seeking out wilderness therapy. You can increase your understanding and take a look at the recent past to identify what you want to **own**. Our hope is that, as you move through this section, you will find yourself less anxious and more committed to the process, even when it feels as if the road ahead is long and arduous.

Chapter 1

Hone Your Understanding: Why Wilderness?

There are many common situations you are bound to face as you head into the journey of wilderness or longer-term residential therapy with your child. As parents confront the uncertainty of what is to come, in order to move forward steadily, we find it very useful to explore answers to the question, "Why wilderness therapy?" For decades, wilderness therapy has grown as an industry and, just like with human development, its progression has included two steps forward and one step back as it solidified an identity as an effective alternative treatment for struggling adolescents and emerging young adults.

It is important to mention here that we have some bias. We are both psychotherapists with extensive careers as wilderness therapists working with adolescents and young adults. We believe wholeheartedly in outdoor behavioral healthcare as a powerful treatment option for children who are not finding ways to thrive with the resources available at home. The questions that burn on the minds of many parents who are on this journey with their children is, "Why should we believe in it, and will it work?"

Let's first consider what we believe is the most universal benefit: going to wilderness therapy gets you into nature, period. Whether you consider yourself a "nature person" or not, it is likely you have relished a moment witnessing natural beauty or slowed down with a deep inhale as you sit on a park bench and look around. Even without getting into the evidence-based research on the effects of the natural world on stress and heart health, you know that it is good for you.

During our days as wilderness therapists, we saw kids whose parents made it clear, and who made it clear themselves, that they were "not outdoorsy at all" and who grew to love the beauty and solace of nature. Additionally, the opportunity to be awe-inspired comes more easily when surrounded by the natural world. The effect of awe-inspiring moments on the brain is a phenomenon that has roughly 20 years of research behind it. According to psychologists, Drs. Dacher Keltner and Jonathan Haidt, who provided us with a conceptual approach to "awe," the emotion awe can arise from a wide range of stimuli characterized by "perceived vastness" and a "need for accommodation". When the experience or stimulus exceeds our expectations in some way, it can provoke an attempt to change our thinking, allowing us to create a need for cognitive realignment that is essential in the effect of awe inspiring moments and experiences.

A recent letter from a child in wilderness therapy to his parents expresses some of this.

Dear Mom and Dad,

I miss you guys so much. Today was very rainy and I did a decent job of keeping my gear dry. Some things we have seen are big horned sheep, a kangaroo mouse by the water jugs, and a den from a ring tailed cat. Another cool thing we saw after we went climbing was a native American pictograph as well as cowboy graffiti. I have been helping out making dinner for my group by the fire and it makes me want to cook for us when I am home. I also have been working on carving spoons for you guys.

When your child is in a wilderness environment, while there are aspects about spending most of their time outdoors that will annoy them, the chance to be up at sunrise, to make a fire without a lighter to get hot water started for their group, and then to look up to see a mama and baby deer wander by, is unlikely to occur at home. Wilderness therapy offers the opportunity to interrupt the potential isolation and over-connectedness to devices to provide more chances to experience the physiological effects of awe.

 **Nugget of Knowledge:** This is an ideal time to consider your own willingness to be exposed to nature, experience moments of awe, and the many other benefits you can receive. Even a 20-minute walk in a city park proves to decrease stress, improve attention, and much more.

The most obvious reason we believe in the power of wilderness therapy is that those who participate in wilderness treatment get the opportunity few have: to abruptly eliminate day-to-day experiences or habits that are not serving them. These day-to-day experiences contribute to feeling stuck, reinforcing unhelpful beliefs, making the same daily des-tructive decisions, and engaging in the same unhealthy rel-ationships. Albert Einstein is credited with saying, "We cannot solve our problems with the same thinking we used when we created them." Getting into a new environment, shifting one's sleep routine, disconnecting from technology and substances so that one can reconnect with oneself and heighten the potential of gaining a new perspective on what life has looked like, all supports our foundational belief in the power of this type of journey.

A driving force that enhances the powerful effects of wilderness therapy and elicits change for individuals is the consistent opportunity for vulnerability and capability. If vulnerability is the state of emotional exposure that comes with a degree of uncertainty and risk and allows for, at a minimum, greater strength, stronger relationships and improved self-acceptance, then wilderness treatment is the place to be to find the courage to experience, grow from, and learn from it.

From the moment an adolescent or a young adult finds themselves in a wilderness program, they start their immediate journey on a path of adaptability and capability. These are powerful skills to **hone** and personality traits to nurture. Wilderness provides daily experiences and opportunities to practice accepting and adjusting to things that one dislikes or doesn't agree with, forcing adaptation throughout the day as one pushes themselves forward while experiencing moment after moment that remind and prove to themself how capable they truly are. This is so powerful that by the end of one's wilderness journey, capability truly becomes part of one's character.

We field many questions about what helps wilderness therapy be effective and recently Tracy, a widowed mom with a young teenage son said, "I just learned that the wilderness therapist is not with my son all of the time. So, if he is still only getting therapy once or twice a week, how is it any different than doing therapy at home?" This one is a common question we answer for parents who are just learning the ins and outs of this treatment modality approach. It is important to know that growth is not all about the wilderness therapist. In addition to the wilderness itself, contributing factors include the peer group and its culture.

The peer group model in wilderness therapy creates the space for peers to explore together, without shame, the stories of their lives they tend to shove into internal dark places when they are with friends from home. The façade worn in the real world fades and, with many peer groups in wilderness, "cool" starts to get redefined by being able to experience and practice vulnerability, delve into one's therapeutic journey, take accountability, and reflect on emotions and behaviors. That type of peer group is hard to recreate and unfortunately is often nonexistent in a home environment. Even when there are peers at home who can offer some resemblance to what we describe, the students in wilderness are not yet able to engage in it until they have the practice.

Supporting all of this work are the paraprofessionals, known as field guides or field staff, who are skilled with group dynamics and in teaching the concrete skills that build competence. Depending on the program your child is in, this could include the map and compass skills needed to get from one site to another, learning to make a fire with a bow drill and learning about the plants and trees used to make a bow drill set. This also includes teaching and practicing executive functioning skills, cooking, communication, emotion management, and problem solving, just to name a few.

The field staff are in close contact with the therapist as they work together to discuss observations made and what behavioral changes to focus on about individuals and the group. In Tracy's case for example, it was important to notice how her son managed the transition into his group and how he interacted with peers around him, as he tended to miss social cues and often cross lines with people at home that he did not seem to know he was crossing. Observing the students during different types of activities, the field staff could report to the therapist when he seemed to read the room well and when he seemed to miss the mark or also what themes in the group seemed to ignite his reactivity.

As he grew through the program and illustrated increased competence in some areas, the field staff and therapist would work together to give him different roles in the day, such as being in charge of cooking for the group, to see where he could practice new skills and get direct support from his field staff when it was more challenging. While cooking might not seem like a big deal, there are many brain-based and executive functioning skills that it involves and the complexities compound when cooking for a group of peers. Organizing, time management, and facing the emotions that come with the inability to please everyone, are a part of each job and aspect of daily life that touch on different areas of brain functioning, which ultimately supports a holistic assessment of a child's development, strengths, and struggles.

While the above are foundational reasons why the leap of faith into wilderness therapy has contributed to the health of families for decades, they do not cover it all. You will learn much more as you go through the process with your child's wilderness program and therapist, and we encourage you to ask questions and advocate for the information you think you need to confidently move forward on this journey with your family.

Rites of Passage for Families & Children

One foundational aspect of the wilderness therapy model is the rite of passage that it provides in a culture where ritualistic milestones have faded into the past. While there is much work that goes into some of our most common societal rites of passages and there is a great feeling of accomplishment by many, there are also the distractions to the depth of the rite of passage with big parties and large gifts that can diminish the rites that one is attempting to claim. The wilderness therapy experience can be a much more accurate rite of passage for many reasons.

Joseph Campbell shaped the concept of "the hero's journey" based on a cross-cultural review of history's myths, legends, and tales to identify common stages in the stories of heroes. Some of the main components include a call to adventure, a separation from your normal life, engaging with a mentor, facing challenges along the way, and returning having identified your inner gifts so that you can offer them to yourself and your community. Simply hearing some of that language, you can already connect the parallels between wilderness therapy and the stages of a hero's journey or a rite of passage.

One wilderness group summarizes that, at their most basic, all rites of passage are characterized by three distinct phases: separation (leaving the familiar), transition (a time of testing, learning and growth), and return (incorporation and reintegration). One of the global facets of this style of rites of passage is the importance of "going without to go within." In order to enhance introspection and the possibility of gaining impactful insight, you go without the comforts and distractions of your day-to-day norm. Imagine trying to meditate with your phone next to you with your notifications on and consider how likely you are to stay attuned internally rather than sneaking a peak or having frustration stirred by the incoming "ding". Our kids have way too many things that they would prefer to be doing and so, getting them away from distraction gives them a chance to go inward with whatever capacity they have.

While the journey through wilderness therapy is a rite of passage, some wilderness programs might also include a solo experience, where your child will have time to themselves and without distractions. From the beginning of this journey, your commitment to this process can also help to facilitate the rite of passage inherent to wilderness therapy, for your child and your family.

Many parents we support report that their children are driven by a poor sense of self, a lack of confidence. This is often the result of children staying inside their comfort zones, avoiding the slightest sense of anxiety, embarrassment, and nervousness, either depleting their competencies, or the awareness of how competent they are, or the opportunity to develop competence. This rite of passage experience will likely come with many "aha" moments of insight as well as opportunities to overcome "I can't" moments.

One of the gifts of the rite of passage experience that wilderness therapy provides is the number of opportunities to face an "I can't" challenge and come out the other side with new beliefs such as, "I can", "I did", "I am willing to try again." To discover one's gifts or character strengths, whether courage, humility, helping others, problem solving, asking important questions, being kind, and more, and then use them to change their life, that is the true nature of the rite of passage. As your child begins to articulate some of these for themselves, we encourage you to uncover your own gifts, what gets in the way of **owning** and **enacting** them, and what you can do to benefit from them more often.

 **Nugget of Knowledge:** Carl Jung who worked closely with Campbell to explore myth and psychoanalysis, espoused, "I am not what happened to me. I am what I choose to become."

As you wade through the feelings about and questions regarding your child's process in treatment, you can implement the H.O.M.E. model by asking, "What questions can I ask my treatment team to gain clarity about my child's experience?" Or, "What gifts of mine can I **own** to bring them forward for myself and my family right now?" One answer to the latter might be, "I am patient and detail oriented and I can use both to gather information over time and help us settle into this new experience."

Chapter 2

Own the Norm of the Recent Past

In order to **hone** skills that can effect change at home, it is integral to first **own** the reality of the norm of your recent past. With perspective and hindsight, you fully comprehend what things looked like, **own** your part, and **hone** the skills for change.

If you are like the majority of parents we support through this process, you likely ask yourself, "How did we get here? How did we fall so far off track?" Whether you have a child struggling with depression, deep anxiety, school refusal and isolation, a child who is neuro-atypical and perhaps diagnosed with Autism Spectrum Disorder, a child who exhibits the dysregulation that comes with bipolar mood swings or substance abuse, or perhaps technology addiction, or any other variation of similar scenarios, the vision that you had of your life when you started a family is most likely different from the reality.

Not only was your original vision different from how things were going but now you're facing another adjustment – having your child out of your home. Consider this experience as a rite of passage for your family; a chance to face the challenges that come with the path toward change. It is important to deeply understand how you got here and to be honest about the details of what it looked like. The goal is that you do everything you can to create change and shape the home you want for yourself and for your family. Identifying what you don't want your home to look like can be a key step in understanding what you do want it to look like.

It is also important to notice what is the same or different about your home with your child away in treatment. What tension or troublesome patterns with your co-parent are remaining? What has changed with one member out of the household? What has not changed?

You Are Not Alone: Naomi & Markus' experience.

Naomi and Markus are the parents of three children aged 15, 18, and 20. As we started our work together, they shared they grew up in relatively functional families. One parent was raised with the expectation of being a high achiever and the other guided by the value of independence, allowing the kids to live their lives as long as they met some reasonable expectations. Naomi and Markus expressed having raised their children in a similar way, encouraging them to find interests and be engaged with the community and perhaps going a little light on at-home chore expectations. They felt secure in their parenting and values, noting that their approach seemed to work for their older two children and that, "our youngest has thrown us for a loop."

Naomi and Markus described their youngest son, who was 15, as having always struggled in school. He fought to sit still, often to the great frustration of teachers and in many ways, they believed that he never felt that he was good enough. He started really acting out at 12, becoming more explosive, especially if they tried to manage his screen time, and by 14 he was smoking pot, had stopped engaging in sports and other things he had been interested in and started to get his energy out by punching holes in walls with even the most reasonable requests.

As Naomi and Markus identified, "It got to the point where we were so exhausted by the nightly battles over technology that we stopped trying to shut things down; he obviously stopped sleeping and his ADHD, anxiety, and suicidal thoughts got worse and worse even though he tried to convince us that having his phone all night was the only thing that helped his anxiety." After they paused to look at the norm that was shaping their home, the effort they had put in to attempt to guide things in a healthy direction for so long, and their pattern of giving up out of exhaustion which they saw was not helping their son, Naomi and Markus make the painstaking decision to reach out for support for their child outside of the home.

Naomi and Markus's story is similar to many families who come our way, who have tried everything they know at home and who engaged as much support as was available in their local area, including academic support for their child's learning challenges, mental health support with local therapists, or partial hospitalization programs for a child who was self-harming or expressing suicidal thoughts or behaviors. We find that many parents, in an effort to do all they can to keep the peace and keep their family intact, let the values with which they wanted to raise their kids fall to the wayside as they live in moment-to-moment survival mode. Whatever your story is, there was likely a "new norm" that took over your household, like a fog moving into your home, infiltrating your clarity with a cloudy layer of confusion and helplessness.

Perhaps you also stopped fighting the battles over technology at night while you took every opportunity to try to preserve the relationship with your child. Perhaps that led to them taking advantage of you in an opportunistic and entitled way or, for some, led to you facilitating learned helplessness by overdoing for them. Maybe you found yourself closed in the home office for longer than you needed to be and closed yourself in the bathroom when your perseverating child followed you around the house until you said yes to their demands. You are exhausted, tired of living in fear and without a clear plan forward and perhaps even refer to moments as "PTSD" (Post Traumatic Stress Disorder) moments from living for too long in a battle zone.

 **Nugget of Knowledge:** You are not alone and there are likely people in your community in the same situation as you who are afraid to talk about it.

Recognizing the Norm: Sharon & Jill's experience.

Sharon and Jill, a couple with two daughters, identified how their younger child's actions took over the mood of the whole home. Jill shared that, even though she thought her situation wasn't worthy of the term, it was accurate to say that she had PTSD every time she came home from work. She described how her heart started to race and that she did not even want to open the door. Sharon tended to be the primary parent throughout the day and would text Jill often, especially when everyone was home through COVID-19, with the challenges she faced with their daughter. Jill described coming home anxious about what she was walking into and heartbroken that they could not simply enjoy any time together.

"We cannot even get her to have dinner with us anymore," Jill shared. "I prepare myself to be bombarded by my exhausted partner with the goings on of the day and prepare myself for whatever role I will be asked to play, which is usually to go upstairs and demand that our daughter shut her technology down, which will lead to her threatening to hurt herself if I don't leave the room. It is so hard to come home to this and I find myself hiding at work and ignoring my partner's texts throughout the day which, of course, is negatively affecting our relationship. Meanwhile, our other child, who still comes to the dinner table, is starting to ask why they have to if their sister can sit in her room doing whatever she wants."

So many of our families share stories you might recognize, highlighting a polarized co-parenting dynamic, with each parent working against the other, one seen as too rigid and the other too lenient, both of them fighting to be more right and get the other "on the same page", rather than seeing the differences as complementary and working together toward a middle ground. Who has the time or the emotional currency for the communication it would take to co-parent well?

It is painful and important to become familiar with the details of what the norm of the recent past was and how it actually became the norm prior to sending your child to treatment. For the health of your child and the survival of your family, you took your first steps into a new norm, the norm of having a child in wilderness therapy. When we addressed this step with Naomi and Markus, they described the uncertainty they felt in the days leading up to bringing their child to a wilderness program and in the week after he was gone. Markus expressed how, as soon as his son was out of the house, he recognized the hole that was left in his absence. His heartstrings tugged and he second-guessed his decision, piling on to his initial skepticism around the financial commitment.

"But Naomi pointed out to me that we were both sleeping better and that I had already spent more time talking to my older children in the last week than I had in a long time," he said. Roughly three days after his son left for wilderness therapy, Markus walked past his room for the first time and noticed the dirty dishes, the hole in the wall, the gaming console and his heart began racing in panic. "I was able to recognize my familiar panic and then took a deep sigh of relief, feeling comforted by the fact that our son was out of the dark hole of an environment he put himself in."

A potentially unpredicted facet of managing this new reality is the internal and external juggle of friends, family, and milestone events your child is not attending. The first step for facing these queries is to have a self-regulation practice and think ahead to develop agreed-upon scripts for your replies. This is important so that you do not take it personally when asked where your child is. Your "script" can simply be the truth, though we recognize that the truth might not be a fit for every family's situation right now.

The complexity can be baffling as we have found when working with families who, for example, have twins, one in wilderness therapy and one at home. No matter your situation, what is most important is that you do your best to replenish your emotional coffers and not deplete them. If you need to preserve energy by avoiding some of these events right now, give yourself that permission. If you desire or are obligated to be in attendance somewhere, determine in advance what is important to you to share and with who. You do not want to wear this new norm with shame if you can avoid it. You have made a decision for the health of your child and your family and, while it comes with heartache, it also opens the door to hope.

Chapter 3

The Acknowledgment of Grief & Loss

As you examined bits of your current norm in the last chapter, you most likely experienced some of your own grief. Often there is grief over the loss of the family you thought you would have and the lives you anticipated with your children. Even prior to deciding that an alternative intervention such as wilderness therapy was needed, you were probably grieving. Through this journey, parents juggle not only their own emotions but also the emotions of the child in treatment, children at home, and also the emotions (or, at the very least, the judgments) of extended family and friends. And now, there is a new grief that you will witness in yourself as a parent, and you will likely hear about how your child, while in a treatment setting, is also experiencing grief. In order to remain steadfast through this, it is important to understand and explore the grief and loss that underlies it all.

Grief has been studied for ages, most notably by Elizabeth Kübler Ross and her contemporary, David Kessler, who identified the stages of grief they witnessed as they supported individuals and their families through loss and tragedy. They identified denial, anger, bargaining, depression, and acceptance and Kessler explored an additional stage of finding meaning. They saw the stages, which are not necessarily linear, as tasks one needed to work through on the path toward acceptance – acceptance of the new reality, the loss, the thing that you could not change. It is through acceptance and finding meaning that one can take forward steps in the new reality, rather than suffering and fighting against it.

For you, there is a big piece of your family puzzle who is no longer in the home. This reality does not come with the pride of being an empty nester who sent their child off to college and now can shamelessly do whatever they want, whenever they want in their day. It is this grief that, in part, contributes to second guessing your decision, as you start to miss her and to reimagine the hopeful possibilities for your family. It is this grief that will compel you to reach out to the program in the first days for information that you most likely already have and it is this grief that will push you to ask one more time if your child can have different food that she likes more, even though she has no food allergies and everyone else is doing just fine. When you receive a letter from your child on day five of their journey that suggests they are ready to come home and are willing to go to therapy every day and spend all of their time with you and ditch all their unhealthy friends, it is the grief that will make you believe it.

Your child's grief will illustrate some of the classic stages of grief. Their grief is over the loss of the life that they had and the control they felt, even as things spiraled out of control. There is a loss of daily comforts–your child who you perhaps battled to shower while at home will complain about not being able to shower. The loss of the comforts will be palpable, not the least of which will be the loss of technology that many in this generation have not experienced life without for some time. He will no longer be in a place where dinner will be brought to him if he refuses to leave the room and join everyone else at the table. The dishes won't be done for him, and the food won't be cooked for him.

And yes, more than these entitlement losses, which may or may not fit your story, there will be a bigger reality check that includes the daily physical challenges while being a part of group of peers who take turns having a bad day, at times refusing to cooperate all while being asked to dig past the surface to examine the things that have been avoided through all the day-to-day distractions at home. The H.O.M.E. model encourages you here to ask questions such as, "What thoughts and feelings can I **own** right now to better understand my grief?" and, "What do I need to **hone** right now to support myself through this?" Perhaps your answer would include practicing self-soothing or developing **mastery** over slowing down so emotions don't take over.

The challenging tasks to process grief aim toward accepting a new reality and this new reality is very tough to accept. If the goal is to earnestly invest in the new reality, which includes the loss, it can take some serious time to get there and there will likely be a lot of effort to avoid it. Parents hear about and read letters from their children who are in denial, angry, and blaming.

- *You should be here, not me. I was just about to do a bunch of makeup work to get caught up in school and you ruined that for me.*
- *Everything was fine; I only smoked pot once and it is legal now and you are overreacting.*
- *You have abandoned me, and I will never forgive you.*

In addition to this, you will likely hear bargaining and about their depression:

- *I will go to tutoring, or, I will go to therapy every day, or, I will ditch my old friends.*
- *I would rather be in jail, at least there is TV there.*
- *I have never been more depressed than I am right now.*
- *You need to come and get me so that I can get better, this place is only making me worse.*

We share these examples not to minimize the reality of your child's experiences, as we have seen these words in letters thousands of times, and we believe that each student believed themselves every time. Just like an addict going through withdrawals, especially if there is mental illness at the root of the problem, your child is on a roller coaster and will take you with them in an "I hate you, don't leave me" sort of way, which is illustrated well in the book, "I Hate You, Don't Leave Me" authored by Jerold J. Kreisman and Hal Straus.

Acknowledging Everyone's Grief: Bryan & Eve's experience.

Bryan and Eve received a letter during the first week of wilderness therapy, from their 17-year-old daughter who, prior to wilderness, was refusing to come home, was engaged in substance use, initiated daily fights with her parents, was self-harming weekly and would threaten self-harm when things were not going the way she preferred.

I need you to know that this is not the place for me. I know I need some support, but I don't need to hike or learn to make fire. I need to be in therapy more often and, even though I refused to go while I was at home, I understand now that it will help me. Many of my problems are also your fault for not giving me the freedoms I wanted. There are also people here with worse issues than mine and I know how to manage my challenges, I just wasn't before. I am dirty and miss my friends and my life. I am ready to be at home and have an idea of what it can look like.

She goes on to propose a plan of doing part-time school so that she can get a job and have time for therapy, along with finding a family therapist, which she previously refused to participate in, and a support group specific to her struggles.

I am sure that the therapists here are good, but I believe there is very little I could get out of this program. My plan is to check myself out a week from today when I turn 18. I will be homeless if you don't pick me up and if that is what you want for me that is fine and you can feel guilty about that or you can pick me up.

Children in wilderness therapy are experiencing loss along with facing fears and challenges that they do not believe they can **master**. The words they use are not just manipulation, as many parents believe, but rather their attempt at self-preservation and avoiding acceptance and change. If they adjust to the new environment and accept the new reality, then they are faced with a mountain of past, present, and future they don't feel ready to face. They too, like you, are experiencing a large amount of uncertainty. It is in the process of accepting the new reality, that you are in the wilderness and the only way out is through, when things get really hard for our kids. Avoiding is easy. Facing is the true warrior's work.

Our job as parent coaches is to encourage you to believe in your child's ability to adapt and to gain important skills and awareness through the process of accepting the new norm and moving forward. Believing in your child's ability to grow through adversity with support around them is a powerful gift. Prioritizing your child's long term success over their short term comfort is a gift. Your power as a parent is to ask questions of the program supporting them, to gather information, to advocate in a wise-minded way, and to bravely engage in your own work to become a solid anchor as your child grows.

Bryan and Eve's daughter completed the program and still talks about it as a life changing experience; she went on to a therapeutic boarding school and continues to thrive after being home for roughly a year. She is just one of thousands of examples of a child's ability to navigate grief and discomfort while finding resilience on the other side.

As you consider how grief and loss are affecting you and your family, we encourage you to also define what it looks like for you to accept, to face the reality, to find your way through and to stand strong in your commitment to this process for yourselves and your family. While doing so, continue to acknowledge and honor your grief and the grief being experienced by every member of your family.

 **Nugget of Knowledge:** While you do not have to minimize your grief by comparing it to the suffering of others, you can remember Helen Keller's message that the world is full of suffering as well as the overcoming of it.

Remember. Reflect. Revisit.

- **Hone** your awareness of the support that wilderness therapy offers and the importance of rites of passage for your kids. Write down questions to ask of your support team to help you gain a clearer picture of what it all looks like.
- **Own** and reflect on your understanding of the unhealthy norm that had taken over your home.
- Accept your grief and loss without letting it take over your decisions.
- Know that you are not alone.

Chapter 4

Standing Strong:
Own Your Commitment

So far, we have touched on the emotions of your new norm and the heartache that comes with it while recognizing the path that led you and your family here. **Honing** your understanding with radical honesty and acceptance can help you to move forward into your next challenge, which is to figure out how to commit to having two feet fully planted in this process. While your child might have two feet physically planted in the desert or the woods, it will take them some time to have two feet into the real work.

This process will likely include several iterations of attempts to get you to bring her home regardless of what real work she completes. In order to be the captain of the ship, it is your responsibility to become the anchor, steadfast through any storm, so that your whole family can move forward from the unhealthy norm that had taken over.

As a parent in this process, you will likely be asked to write a letter to your child in wilderness therapy that directly states your commitment. You have examined the unhealthy and perhaps unsafe lifestyle that was your child's world prior to wilderness therapy, and you are committed to not allowing that to be anyone's norm any longer. Tracy wrote,

Adam, part of me is sad to write this letter and part of me feels relief to share what has been a burden on my heart. You are an amazing kid. I love you more than anything in the world. You were on a destructive path. Your choices not only affected you negatively but those around you, mainly me. I could not bear living with your actions anymore.

As this message becomes clear to your child, that the only way out is through, you will notice how they shift focus from "get me out" to some version of, "fine, what do I need to do?" As this shift occurs, we encourage you to ask yourself the same question. "What do I need to do to

…ensure we don't go back to the norm of the recent past?"

…recover some equilibrium for myself?"

…better understand what role I played and what role I would prefer to play?"

…communicate my commitments in a clear and consistent way?"

Consider for a moment how you would answer these questions. Your child perhaps is in a program that has levels to move through and milestones to accomplish to move forward through those levels. You do not have a level system set out for yourself or clear milestones, nor do you have the luxury of taking 10+ weeks off from your normal day-to-day to get to the bottom of all this and develop new habits. Your child will be steeped in their therapeutic work 24-7, learning a new language in a way, which, rest assured, they will use for their own growth and to call you out on yours. As you shape your healthy rhythm, make sure you carve out time to anchor into the process with both feet.

How will you know when you have two feet in? Likely after a couple of calls with your child's primary therapist, your trust in the program will increase and you will experience some relief, knowing that your child is safe and in good hands. This will certainly increase your ability to commit to this process and you will notice a change in the questions you are asking and the concerns you have. You will, perhaps begrudgingly, accept that your child can more than survive even if they are pooping in a hole outside, aren't allowed to be out of sight of the staff without making some noise to ensure your child is safe and still nearby, and even if they have to eat rice, beans, and nut butter as staples.

If the program supporting your child has a parent curriculum of some sort, one way to have two feet in is to find a rhythm for chunking away at your own homework. It is very important that you, each time you ask if your child is completing their work in the wilderness, make sure to look in the mirror and ask the same question of yourself. While your day-to-day might still be full and busy, you have one child out of the home and as such, more time to do this work than you will when they come home. It is also hugely important to make time for the other children in the home if you have them.

Even with a sibling away in treatment, at home they will still notice how much of the room's air that sibling of theirs takes up. Between weekly calls, letter writing, and working to understand everything you are learning, it will be amazing how much time you will put toward that child. The kids at home need your time too, you know this already, so no excuses... role model the commitment, carve out the time, do your work.

Chapter 5

Learn & Hone a New Communication

As your trust in the program and as your commitment increases, so will your ability to skill build, such as through communication. To **hone** your communication as you walk this parallel journey with your child, it will take **owning** your strengths and struggles with radical honesty and the willingness to learn new communication styles. This matters too much to disregard or ignore. You will be able to assess those through letter writing and receiving, through the teachings of the program about tools such as active listening, and through putting your co-parenting communication under a microscope. Be gentle with yourselves and with each other and just keep trying; on the path to **mastery**, giving up is the only obstacle.

The Art of Letter Writing

During your child's stay in wilderness therapy, you will be invited into a weekly rhythm of letter writing to and from your child, another valuable aspect that supports the growth of the youth in treatment and with the whole family is the letter writing process.

In conversation with parents, we like to remind them, especially when it can be overwhelming, that wilderness therapy is offering them and their child the ability to engage in the art of letter writing. The adolescents and young adults participating in a wilderness experience and their parents are introduced or reintroduced to the art and reminded that it is an art because they have to practice for it to become natural – very similar to the art of parenting. The art of writing can bring relief, peace, clarity, joy, and numerous other emotions.

Your child might refuse to write to you at times and the therapist supporting your family will offer suggestions regarding how to respond, or not. But the key to this aspect of the program we like to point out is the time it takes to write and receive letters. There is a delay in writing and receiving, especially when letters are snail mailed and not emailed, and you will likely have the opportunity for both. Many parents note the frustration of the timing of letters, as you and your child will write letters simultaneously and thus not be able to respond directly nor immediately each time. The act of slowing down communication is hugely important as you learn about your communication style, the communication style of your child, and how to shift communication in ways that fit your family's needs. Consider how much of your communication with your children is "right now"; delayed gratification is a thing of the past and unfortunately, this current state of being has many negative effects on our development and in our relationships.

Reacting to and writing letters presents a great opportunity to assess where you are on the H.O.M.E. continuum. This process can start on the roller coaster of emotion based on receiving "good" or "bad" letters from the child in the field. This can also happen with updates from your wilderness therapist about your child's week. One week you might get one letter that has a positive tone, maybe stating that your child understands your decision about wilderness therapy and is committed to learning and you might feel like you are past the big barriers. The next week, after having normal conflict within their group, the tone may shift toward "get me out of here this place is BS and everyone is mean." It is important you try to avoid getting on the emotional roller coaster and placing black-and-white meaning (things are good or bad, for example) from one letter to the next so that you are better prepared to accept the reality that there will be ups and downs and both are okay.

Often, children make parents think everything is urgent and parents respond in kind, typically to the detriment of all. Slowing down communication through letter writing can help increase awareness of healthy and unhealthy patterns of communications, including situations that might trigger a reaction, rather than a response. Through letter writing, you develop more intentional communication that can be utilized and implemented when face to face with your child again.

A key role you play is to hold up the mirror for your child, to push them to see the past, not with the intention to shame them but with the hope they can better understand what to learn from. Many wilderness programs, for example, ask parents to write a letter that highlights the emotional impact that their child had on themselves and on others around them. This generally is referred to as an impact letter, a letter of concern, an intervention letter, or a placement letter, and it is typically challenging for a parent to write.

While parents are desperate for their children to better understand themselves and change their behaviors, they are equally desperate to protect their children and ensure their happiness. As such, a letter that highlights the challenges from the recent past can seem like something that is intended to hurt or shame. This is far from the truth and the shaping of this letter requires care and support from others. As a piece of the rite of passage model, in order to move forward with new eyes and into a new future, it is important to understand from others' perspectives what it is you are moving on from. Especially for our teens and young adults who often claim that everything was fine and that it is the parents who need to be in wilderness therapy, it is vastly important that they have the opportunity, without distraction, to hear others' experiences of them.

You will likely have opportunities for phone calls with your child in wilderness therapy and you will be invited to at least one visit to the field. Your wilderness therapist will help you prepare for those based on how things are going at the time. These are additional opportunities to move from letter writing to more face to face experiences that encourage you to show up with curiosity, continue to practice your new communication skills, and to make your own observations of yourself and your child.

These observations get to include your awareness of yourself in these moments with your child which can include asking yourself:

What buttons of mine still get pushed? What buttons of others do I push? In what new ways am I responding? What reactions do I have that I would like to keep working on?

To put the H.O.M.E. model of self-assessment into place, you can identify a few moments where communication stirred discomfort, for you or for another with whom you were communicating.

Ask yourself: *To help this situation go a bit more smoothly, was there something I needed to* **hone** *(sharpen understanding of),* **own** *(claim),* **master** *(practice), or* **enact** *(put into place)?*

The opportunities to enhance your communication are abundant, as long as you pay attention and stay honest with yourself and each other.

A New Communication

Communication is how we impart and exchange knowledge, opinions, thoughts, emotions, and perceptions. For some of you, this journey will be about learning new styles of communication, for others the journey will first start with learning how to communicate, which is more complex than simply talking. Some of us are over-communicators and some of us are under-communicators; some of us think out loud while others process internally before they share what they are thinking. Finding out where you land is a good starting point. Knowing what your broader strengths and struggles are is also key, both with listening and expressing.

When you have a child in treatment, steeped in lessons about the power of language and becoming an expert with these new skills, you might get a run for your money when you are asked to communicate thoughts and feelings with developmentally-appropriate transparency.

The more we communicate, the fewer assumptions we make; the less we communicate, you guessed it, the more assumptions we make, often with negative impact on relationships. We all know what happens when we ASS-U-ME and, part of your work while you engage in this treatment process, is to make sure your feelings, thoughts, and commitments are not left to assumption. Just as letter writing is an art that requires practice, so too is most communication.

It is amazing how miscommunication and reactivity continue to occur, even slowed through letter writing, and this is a great opportunity to understand common areas of misunderstanding and how they come to be.

Much of communication is automatic, which then becomes habit-forming, moving us away from using thoughtful and intentional language that leads to more effective communication. Wilderness treatment has been around for over 30 years, and in its evolution, a few concepts have stayed consistent: letter writing and the "I feel" statement. The power of an "I" statement to support this process cannot be overstated. An "I" statement provides clarity – it can speak to how you define yourself and your values, it empowers you to have ownership of your ideas, your thoughts, feelings, and beliefs, and to speak your truth. It helps you counter the tendency to blame others or simply to focus on what others could or should be doing.

"I feel worried when you come home late," can lead to a very different conversation than, "You keep coming home late and it's so selfish." It can feel forced at first but over time, you will learn to make it yours and find language that is true to you, claiming your feelings with clarity rather than blaming. Using "I" statements and specific language can transform your daily connections and your relationships, which makes it imperative to pay more attention to your words.

A letter from a parent who has been practicing "I feel" statements might read:

I received your recent letter of accountability and I feel a bit overwhelmed with everything you shared as I was caught off guard to learn how much I was unaware of. I have often felt helpless about the best ways to support you through your challenges and the brave step you took to share all of this helped me to feel hopeful that we might be able to communicate more as we work together on this journey.

Culturally, we are often fast thinkers and fast talkers, and we tend to be less conscious of the words we are using and what they are communicating. In Don Miguel Ruiz's "The Four Agreements", he identifies, "be impeccable with your word" as one of his guiding principles. A great way to be more impeccable, to increase the richness of your communication, and model new communication, is to not only use the "I" statements but also to better identify if you are communicating an emotion, a thought, or a belief. The journey of wilderness therapy, in part, helps to increase the emotional intelligence (EI) of families and you can contribute to that through developing and increasing your own EI. The ability to identify the emotion that underlies your reaction, claim it, and articulate it offers transparency, vulnerability, and modeling that can shape the tone of your home.

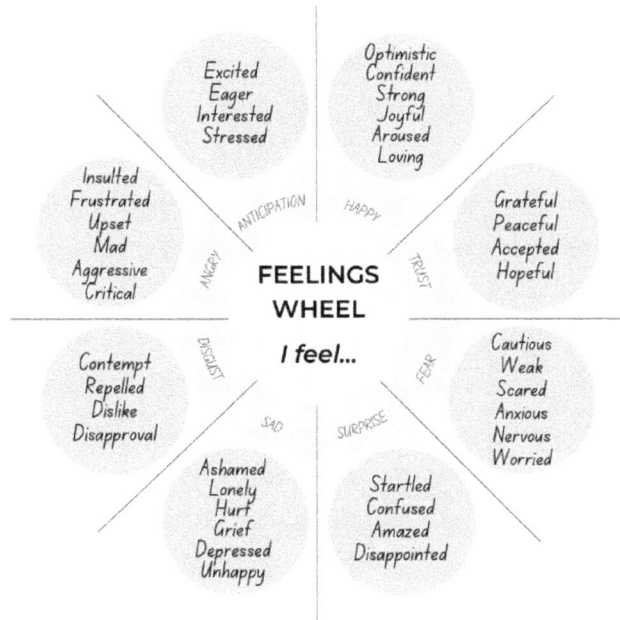

Based on the Feelings Wheel developed by Leadskill.com.

As you explore your communication styles, keep in mind the role active listening plays. When have you walked away from a moment and truly felt listened to? What was it the listener did to help? Nonverbal communication and active listening contribute to the quality of an interaction and the chance that participants in a conversation walk away feeling heard. Being an active listener means that you can quiet your own internal narrative, regulate your emotions, show genuine interest in someone's stance, and reflect.

Reflection is a part of the active listening interchange and it's simply an acknowledgment that you were listening. Reflection can bring clarity and confirm you received the message the person was trying to convey accurately. This is the place for curiosity, being genuinely interested in another's experience and letting go of the need for factual accuracy based on your perspective.

 **Nugget of Knowledge:** While there is research to counter the decades-old belief that 98% of communication is nonverbal, the fact is that it still plays a big role. Notice and **own** your eye rolls and deep sighs as often as you notice those of your children.

Practicing new communication. Lev's experience.

Lev reached out for support after receiving a letter from his child in treatment. The family was working to understand and support their daughter's gender identity, assigned male at birth, as she explored it herself.

I have always felt different and have known and told you for years, since I was five, that I was not a boy and you never listened.

Lev already felt out of his element a bit, behind the times with understanding gender identity. Further, his experience of his child was different from what she was reporting.

"How do I respond to that?" Lev asked. "It just isn't true. She mentioned nothing about this to us until about a year ago, so I don't know why she thinks she has been talking about this with us since she was five."

Through the parent coaching process and trying to use H.O.M.E. to guide himself forward, Lev asked, what can I **own** in order to respond and not react? And what concepts can I **hone** and **enact**, to help me better understand my role here? We identified his emotion, his curiosity about her version of reality and responding to the emotion of the expression rather than the details. We additionally worked to **hone** an understanding of the intention of the communication. Rather than working to push his daughter toward a concrete goal that Lev felt was important, which previously included trying to get her to agree with "the real facts", Lev agreed that the more important intention for right now was to build attachment and connection.

It must have been so hard to feel different for so long and to feel like no one was listening to you. I am thankful that we are going through this process now to learn how to work together and communicate better with each other and I hope that we both keep trying.

When Lev received the response to his letter from his daughter, it was clear that she felt truly heard and dad recognized how, if he had focused on arguing the different experience of the "facts", he might have missed the opportunity.

Chapter 6
Supporting Siblings at Home

Navigating Siblings at Home: John & Rebecca's experience.

John and Rebecca's child was starting his second week in a wilderness therapy program when we first spoke. While they presented much they wanted to work through, one situation that they were not prepared for was the silent treatment by their 17-year-old daughter at home.

"Even though there were nights when she would not leave her room because her brother was so out of control, she is still so angry that we made this decision to get him support outside of our home. She literally has stopped talking to us except to share the negative press she found on wilderness therapy, pulling out all the stops to try and make us feel terrible. We also know that she is unaware of everything that was truly going on with her brother that led us to make the decision which makes it all the more difficult."

If you have other children at home and, depending on the quality of the relationship with their sibling in treatment, you are likely going to have a slew of other emotions that you need to support inside your home. Siblings at home might give you the silent treatment like in Rebecca and John's case. They might be confused and stand up for their sibling in treatment, arguing and minimizing on their behalf, potentially not knowing the full extent of the unhealthy norm you all were in. Some siblings could not be happier to have this change. They might breathe deeply with relief, glad to get a break from the war zone in which they were an innocent bystander who found their safe haven closed away in their rooms. They might act like nothing at all is different as they go about life in their own worlds.

Some siblings who experience relief or are glad their sibling is out of the home may also grapple with guilt about how they feel. Siblings at home might have lots of questions and some might act like nothing has happened. There are increased opportunities for you to be intentional with them and it might be attention they are not used to receiving. Much of your time, focus, and energy will still be geared toward the child in treatment and that will be clear to the kids at home, which could augment any resentment they were feeling.

This is their grief and loss as well. They might have lost their scapegoat, their best friend, their antagonist, their pot dealer, their confidant, their partner in chore responsibilities. On top of the grief over the loss of the sibling, there could be confusion alongside the reality check that they have parents who will intervene and use out of home treatment as a resource. To manage this, they could tap into the naysaying resources on the internet that point out the problem areas with wilderness therapy but they won't also track down all of the stories of grateful parents and children who report wilderness therapy having saved their lives.

For parents, start by getting a finger on the pulse of where things stand with the kids at home. And, while the quiet, athletic, "A" student who takes care of themself and is ready for school on time without prompt has been a blessing, don't let them slide under the radar anymore. If siblings are already in therapy, encourage them and their therapists to talk about this transition. They have thoughts and feelings about everything, and they have depended on their top quality coping skills to get by and stay out of the way.

Carve out one-on-one time to check in with everyone and be prepared to be a solid vessel if they are willing to unload. You might hear things you don't agree with or that do not represent the full picture or may seem attacking and your only job is to be the strong-sided vessel that can hold it all in the moment. Then, schedule an appointment with your therapist, or go on a walk with a friend or your partner, or someone who you can unload on as well to get the perspective you need to keep showing up for your kids at home.

"I wish my kid was willing to unload so much that I needed to be a vessel. I can't even get her to say anything other than 'I'm fine'." We hear this a lot, too. So, be patient. Don't fill in the words for her or press her that there must be something she thinks or has to say. Just keep chipping away at it. Maybe the invitation is through a text. "Give me five words about what you are thinking about all of this and then I'll stop bugging… until next week. :)" Or even offer a multiple choice question that they can answer and let that be enough for now. If they are not in therapy or willing to give it a try, now might be a good time, even if just for a couple of months to have someplace that is just theirs to appropriately unload and get outside perspective.

There are two main aspects to manage in these interactions while you support siblings at home through this – the external communication with the kids and the internal experience of it all for yourselves. Considering ways to manage the former, it is important to allow siblings at home to experience their feelings without trying to convince them of your perspective. One communication strategy we encourage is "I hope" statements, which allow you to be clear about your feelings and attempt to redirect your child's thinking, encouraging more flexibility in theirs.

"This is really hard for us, too, and we hope that one day you can understand where we are coming from."

If she responds with, "I won't understand it because it is abusive and wrong," it is important to avoid the tit for tat that could ensue and to accept her stance.

"It's difficult to know that you see it that way and we know we can't change how you feel about it."

Internally, the emotions of your children at home could cause your guilt to flare, your fear to surface, and your desperation to lead to overwhelm. These are the times when self-awareness and self-regulation are important. The push-back from siblings at home often stirs patterns of anxiety and second-guessing. While it is important to notice it, it is also important not to give the steering wheel over to it. To captain your ship, you can take the challenges to your decisions and look at them as a researcher and in a wise-minded way. Why does her pushing bother me so much? What do I know about the new norm of the recent past that led to our decision? Why is it important to me that she understands or agrees with where we are coming from?

Siblings at home might be invited into the treatment process first through letter writing. Especially if you are trying to involve them in the impact or intervention letter process, this can be a challenge. It is important to consider the stability and coping skills of the child at home who you are asking to engage in this way. If they do not have much support, it might not be the right move to enforce their participation. You can always offer it as an invitation and, if the child in treatment is asking them to write, it can still be a choice. We were once offered the opportunity to have an email correspondence directly with a sibling at home who wanted to write a letter, and this is what we shared with them:

If you could say anything to your sister, what would you want to say? What would you want her to hear when you think about your relationship, when you think about growing up together and when you think about behaviors or actions that she has chosen and how they may have affected you? Be specific about the behaviors and be specific about how you feel.

A good trick to communicating in these types of letters is to practice "I" statements. I think... follow those two words with a thought, I believe... follow those two words with a belief and I feel... the NEXT word to follow needs to be a feeling. I feel angry, I feel disappointed, I feel hurt, I feel relieved. In the end, if you are open to it, share your hopes, what do you hope for the relationship, what do you hope for your sister as she invests in this therapeutic work. Potentially, if you're comfortable I would also consider telling her what you need from her to move forward in your relationship.

While your family at home is attempting to find their way with one member away in treatment, we often suggest you institute a "What's Going Well" meeting to get your family in the habit of it and to create a culture of positive comm-unication. It's easy to hyperfocus on the hard parts and often kids at home need permission to be happy and still enjoy their day, even when Mom and Dad are clearly struggling. We help parents identify the questions that matter to them to ask in these meetings, which can be as quick as 10 minutes.

Questions could be: "What did I do to help my life go well this week?", "What did our family do well this week?", "What did I see someone else in the family do well this week?" Some families have the bandwidth to address what didn't go well and what they want to improve on for next week and others do not.

We encourage you to, at the very least, do one round where everyone shares a skill or trait they exercised through the week to help things go well.

Involving siblings at home needs to be thoughtfully encouraged with respect for choice and clarity about options they have. Unrelated to their thoughts regarding wilderness therapy, you are going to have more bandwidth than before to offer to them, which doesn't always turn out to work in their favor. Things they say and choices they make that have gone unnoticed in the past six months might get more attention. Be aware of this and try to notice their strengths out loud as often as you notice the struggles.

Remember. Reflect. Revisit.

- Commit with two feet in to better support your family through this journey.
- Increase your understanding of your communication tendencies and engage a different approach, such as with "I" statements, through the art of letter writing.
- Keep an eye on the ways siblings at home are faring through the transition of having a child in a treatment environment.

PART 2

Own & Master:
The Sacred Pause

Part 2
Own & Master: The Sacred Pause

This section invites you to prioritize YOU – to take a deep look at what matters most to you to put time toward shaping your life, ultimately impacting the tone of your home. We encourage you to come back to this part of the book time and again, when you need the reminder to **own** and **master** putting yourself first.

In our description of rites of passage for children and families, we touch on the hero's journey concept. The hero's journey always includes an invitation, a call to adventure, which one can refuse or accept. This section is your invitation. If accepted, the journey you then embark on can lead you to feel awakened, as though you had several years of counseling and inspiring "aha" moments. Your journey may even lead you to sing from the rooftops that you are ready to take on whatever comes your way with faith in yourself and belief that you will be at your best when you can and have a "let's keep trying" attitude when you can't. We want you to walk away from this section feeling like your role in shaping the tone of your household, the tone of your life, is as solid as it can be.

We invite parents to pause because life moves too quickly, this work is too important, and your family too valuable, to not take this sacred pause. When we refer to a pause, we simply suggest you break from the busyness and the problem solving so you can invest time in deepening your understanding of yourself. In our work, we find that parents are often wrapped up in work and managing the day-to-day and, even with the reality check of having a child in wilderness therapy, many parents keep moving along with their daily lives, often only carving out time for the weekly calls, for letter writing, and maybe to look at an assignment or two from the wilderness therapist. This is not because parents don't care or because parents think the child in treatment is the only one who needs to do all the work.

Often, parents don't pause because the lives they lead are full and busy and it is challenging to carve out time for other things. And so, the sacred pause. Sacred because it is time dedicated to a higher purpose, looking deep within, to discover who you really are and where you want to be. When we are forced to pause in our life, reflection can occur and the opportunity to implement change follows.

The sacred pause is an invitation for you to **own** and **master**. We want you to **own**, with radical honesty, all of your stuff or at least bits of it. Your baggage, your feelings, your needs, your strengths, your weaknesses, your communication style, the good, bad, and ugly. This is the time for you to make a list of all the things you probably could benefit greatly from talking with a therapist about and make sure that you are looking at how those affect the tone of your home, your interactions with others, your life.

Maybe take an actual pause here to put a few things on your list that you might want to delve into with your therapist.

We want you to **master** awareness, both within yourself and of those around you. **Master** your willingness to be vulnerable, the courage to receive feedback, your responses and intentional rhythm so that the foundation to which your child returns is solid and clear. You will not become some perfect therapeutic robot of a person – and who would really want that anyway? That is not the goal of **mastery**. The H.O.M.E. continuum, includes intentional practices, aware-ness, feedback, and learning. You might not get a response just right, but you will have **mastered** the ability to think about it, look at the pros and cons of your approach and alter for next time if necessary. Through **owning** your part and **mastering** new ways, you will stop plodding along in the same way you have been, and you will carve a new path. We, this book, the therapist working with your child, can all guide you and walk alongside you, but you are the one who must take the action.

Nugget of Knowledge: Part of accepting the invitation to take a deep look at what matters most to you is to find words or phrases that keep you focused. By simply stating, "I will accept the invitation," you are offering yourself the reminder that you deserve this time to prioritize yourself.

Chapter 7

It's Time to Own

The pace at which you move from your time with your child's wilderness therapist, learning about your child, understanding more about your relationship and your family system into needing to think about what comes next, can be experienced like whiplash–it feels enormously fast to many. As such, parents might miss out on this opportunity to "marinate" as they say, to really reflect and understand where you came from, what you have gained since the start of this process, and what it means to you. In order to **own** your part in shaping a new tone at home, you have to be willing to carve out time to marinate. Be clear, taking ownership is different than taking blame. There is no one at fault, there are simply aspects that, if **owned** with confidence, not shame, can empower you as you move forward.

Ideally, your child would see their treatment experience as a journey that is not just about getting out of a supportive and intensive treatment experience but rather that it's about using the time, the teachings, and the tools to stay out and find out how to thrive wherever they might be in their life. We would hope they see it's also about consistently practicing new, healthy skills for managing old familiar challenges.

And so, for parents who are supporting their child and family through treatment interventions, challenging emotions, and difficult decisions, it is equally important you take on this ideal messaging you want your child to have. Further, it's important to determine what you need to **own** to be able to thrive and what skills you need to sustain in order to be the warriors your children and family need. To truly immerse yourself in this process, we encourage you to carve out a consistent period of time each week to sit in reflection, in whatever way works for you, and identify what you are learning about yourself thus far in your journey with your child in treatment that will help you continue to thrive.

The simple yet oh-so complex question from the H.O.M.E. model to help you reflect is: what about me, my past, and how I live my life can I **own**, either to celebrate or to create change, in order to shape my life with more awareness and shape the tone of my home? Let's start by looking at and **owning** some of the things that might be impacting the ways you captain your ship. Honesty with yourself is the tool that can help you the most and, before you move forward, it is vital to look at what you are moving on from and what you want to keep hold of and cultivate. Who are you as a role model? Where do you want to be and what help do you need getting there? Be honest with yourself—what do you blame on your kid, on life's situations, on yourself, on your co-parent? With two eyes wide and your whole heart open, have a willingness to explore some of these subjects:

- **Own** your communication style
- Know your strengths and struggles
- Know your tendencies and patterns
- **Own** your unhealthy habits
- Identify what is amazing about you

- Examine how you express judgment/opinions/beliefs and how do you respond when receiving any of these from others
- Identify the role you play for your family
- Identify the role you want to play
- Identify the role you do not want to play
- Explore your co-parents' strengths and struggles
- Uncover what you need from your co-parent that can help you to be a successful co-parenting partner
- Know the value in their perspective and approach
- Know the value in your perspective and approach

We understand it is easier said than done and that you might need to feel very stable in order to delve into even one of those questions. The experience of trauma – big "T" trauma such as the death of a parent and little "t" trauma such as bullying, both of which can have devastating impact – can make this sort of exploration challenging. Some people have experienced trauma and have not yet engaged intentionally in therapy to learn how the effects interface with various areas of life. Just as you are encouraging your child to "go deep", so too, can you. If you know or believe you might have a past that affects your relationships and you don't have a therapist, go get one. When parents dive in and address what it is they are bringing to the dyad, it allows couples and co-parenting teams the space to support one another in navigating the world around them which includes how to handle parenting your children.

Nugget of Knowledge: Action steps are a must if you want to make genuine change.

Exercise

Take a pause here to identify a few of the bulleted questions and subjects aforementioned, or some you are already chewing on, and write them down. Carve out time, perhaps even 15 minutes right now, to write down the questions and the answers that come to you.

Try these.

What do you model to your children?

What do you blame on your (child, co-parent etc.)?

Identify the role you play for your family and what role you want to play.

Your turn…

Unfortunately, it's part of our humanity to distract ourselves from our deep personal work with technology, with our work lives, or by constantly focusing on others. This takes place because many of us have trauma, little or big, that underlies the more surface emotions, behaviors, and interactions that one is being asked to examine. Many of the parents we support have worked on and off throughout their lives to better understand the impacts of their family of origin, the family they were raised in, and often the place where they learned to become who they are. Once they do, they recognize, through personal work and evolution, the importance of identifying changes to be made to who that person is.

Taking Ownership: Melissa's experience.

Melissa chose questions early on in our time together to tie in throughout the parent coaching work: *What aspects of how I was raised did I appreciate and want to incorporate in my parenting, and which do I want to not incorporate? How will being thoughtful about this change how I show up with my family?* As she received feedback from her child's wilderness therapist and investigated in our coaching sessions how that feedback related to the above questions, her own "aha" moments started to surface.

"I finally understand my tendency to reassure and rescue my kid and that it is due to feeling like there was no one on my side to support me when I was growing up," she explained. "Growing up, I was expected to figure it out on my own, not to ask for help because then I was seen as a burden, and I was often expected to take on extra work around the house without much validation for all that I was doing. My father was a functioning alcoholic who hid himself in work and with friends, and my mother had three of us to support and she was full of resentment. It never occurred to me that I had gone too far to the other end of the spectrum and had kept my child from truly learning to do anything for themself. They struggled to do anything without me."

When you accept the invitation to **own**, you can intentionally and ferociously carve out time to deepen your self-awareness, increase your understanding of the relationship dynamics around you, strengthen your foundation, and shape the tone of your home. You can further **master** your world by identifying what is important to you and immersing yourself in the process of understanding what you have control over. Let this section help you develop a clearer understanding of the skills you need and want to **hone**, to confront the challenges in front of you, and to gain a better understanding of the need for change and evolution in yourself, your relationships, and your parenting skills. Allow this section to assist you in highlighting skills and strategies, bringing you greater clarity and confidence in yourself as a person and as a parent.

You don't have to love motivational gurus to value the sentiment, if you want to change your life, you need to control the one thing you can: the meaning you place on things. **Master** this. Move from guilt, fear, and self-blame into self-care, confidence, and contentment. Take all the emotion you have about your situation and put it toward yourself so you can show up renewed and with restorative practices, habits, and increased awareness. Claim what you have control over and keep reading to see what else you can **master**.

Restore Your Rhythms & Routines

A predictable and consistent rhythm is one of the main pillars of wilderness therapy and longer-term residential treatment that can positively affect physical, mental, emotional, spiritual, and social health.

Too often we become wrapped up in the busyness of our lives and much of our time is given away to support the lives and schedules of others. Between managing kids' schedules, perhaps taking care of aging parents, responding to work ob-ligations, and needs of friends or other family, it might stir up deep belly laughter, followed by a grieving sigh, to consider reshaping your routine for yourself.

The fact is, we often have routines, but they can tend to be unhealthy. As you **hone** your understanding of your own daily habits, you want to observe:

- how you spend your time in ways that feel productive and ways that feel restorative, which are not mutually exclusive,
- how you waste time,
- how you use time effectively,

- how much time you spend anxious or negative,
- how often you cultivate gratitude, and
- how you care for your physical, emotional, mental, and spiritual needs.

The next step is to find small ways to set yourself up for success and create change in your routine to intentionally include ways to replenish. The simple act of committing even 30 minutes to a healthy lunch each day can decrease stress and increase a positive sense of self.

One simple way you can reshape your routine is to notice a passing moment of joy. This moment could be enjoying the colors in a sunset, the laughter of a child, or even just getting Wordle on the second attempt; whatever brings you even a passing smile, take note. We tend to give away much time to the moments that are not so gratifying, and our brains need us to fight back by noticing the delightful moments, too. We need a new rhythm that invites celebration and that is restorative.

Additionally beneficial is the act of noticing when you describe an event, related or unrelated to parenting, as "terrible" when a more complete truth might have been that there were not-so-great moments along with some neutral moments and even some positive moments. The more you ensconce a story with the negative moments in its retelling, the more likely your brain is to feel depleted and remember the event as wholly negative. If instead you can describe an event more fully, "well, there were some not so great bits but also some pretty decent ones as well," the more content your brain is, the more content the memory of that event will be and the more soothed your stress hormones will be in the moment and when you recall the event later. The habit of changing the lens through which you describe events can be **enacted** on the path to shaping restorative rhythms.

Celebrating moments of joy, carving out time to notice, out loud, the things that are going great, can help you along the way. What about your life helps you love it? Is there anything that can change, in your daily rhythm or otherwise, that can healthfully enhance your enjoyment? If stress is primarily captaining your ship, what emotions can you cultivate, through your actions and choices, that can help you captain with a different tone? There is always something you can do, even if some aspects are out of your control.

Exercise

Take time to identify aspects of your routine that drain you and identify small steps you can take to add replenishing moments.

Draining aspects of my routine that I can change.	New routine that is achievable.
Cooking dinner nightly	*Commit to 2 nights a week bringing food in, going out or using a quick frozen meal*
Attempting to fit in daily workout classes at the gym that is 30 minutes away	*Creating space every day for movement, even a 15 minute walk around the neighborhood*

Your turn…

Mastering a restorative rhythm is a great way to role model that being an adult is desirable, which we espouse because it is important for our kids to want to grow up, as anxiety about growing up is pervasive. Additionally, modeling is a key guiding principle with parenting, as we have the opportunity to be the adults we hope our children grow to become.

You live a busy and full life, and it is in the five-minute passing moments that you can incorporate new rhythms. There are many ways to reestablish your personal rhythm that do not require having all of the free time in the world. It can be beneficial to first identify what is important to you. Do you know what you need in your life, short of quarterly vacations, to feel restored? Perhaps you need time in nature, time at the gym, time tending to your yard or garden, in a yoga class or playing basketball with the guys. Perhaps you need interaction with friends or to be engaged in service work in your area. Even the simplicity of implementing a consistent morning or evening routine that feels good to you can contribute to restoration.

Dr. Dan Siegel developed the Healthy Mind Platter, identifying daily essentials to enhance one's brain and overall wellness which include:

- **Focus Time:** when we closely focus on tasks in a goal-oriented way;
- **Playtime:** when we allow ourselves to be spontaneous or creative;
- **Connecting Time:** when we take time to connect with others;
- **Physical Time:** moving our bodies;
- **Time In:** the time we take in quiet internal reflection;
- **Downtime**: the time in non-focused relaxation; and
- **Sleep Time:** when we sleep and give our brain the rest it needs.

Consider implementing a Healthy Mind Platter and ask yourself which areas you are consistently incorporating into your day or week and which areas might need more attention.

Parents in general, and especially those with a child in treatment, spend quite a bit of time focusing on their child's schedule and the routine they expect their child to take on in order to sustain growth and wellbeing. Those schedules often include areas from the mind platter. And so, if the routine is valuable for our kids, it is equally valuable for ourselves.

The Healthy Mind Platter

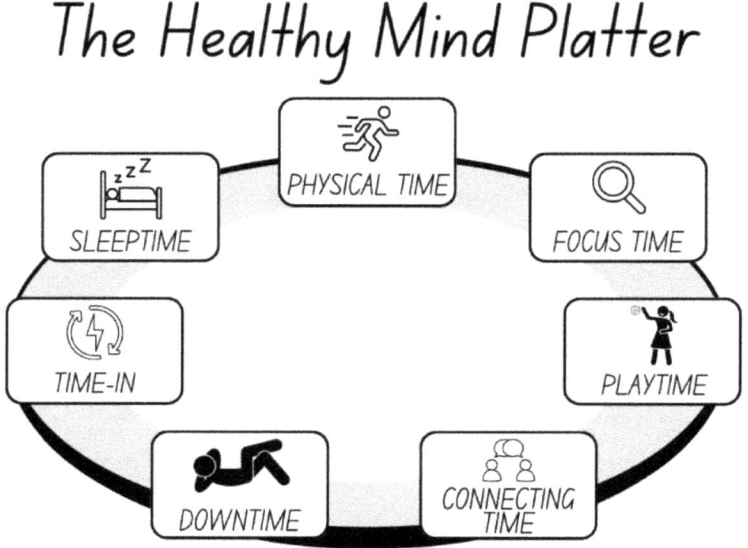

Based on The Healthy Mind Platter developed by David Rock and Daniel J. Siegel.

Reset Your Intentions

To shape a healthy personal rhythm, it is vital to clarify when you are living with intention and when you are distracting yourself.

Living with intention can be defined by asking yourself: *How do I want to show up today and why is that important to me? Or, how do I want to treat myself and others in the next two hours?*

The objective of being more intentional is to **own** how you show up, to be thoughtful of the meaning you place on things and to shape your experiences with whatever control you have. Our intentions have the power to shape our relationships, through communication and connection. And, intentions *without* actions don't get us far while actions without intention can elicit negative consequences.

Let's examine the positive effects of adding intention, or shifting intention, with a common parenting style, which we like to call, the "to do lister". The intention of the "to do lister" parenting style is to prioritize accountability and keep things on track in the way they think is best. The "to do lister" is a parent who hyper-focuses on the to-do lists and can end up prioritizing that over relationship and connection. Too often, this parent pushes to have things done at their pace and in their way and frustration can build quickly with the predictable lack of follow through on the part of their child.

Of course, this role can develop due to experience after witnessing your child's procrastinating and forgetting. And, when the child expects that their accountability "buddy," in this case, their parent, is going to be there constantly to remind them, they are less likely to develop the self-directed approach that we hope they will. The negative impacts on these interactions are all too common with this parenting approach, especially as parents who take this approach often imply, "you are not capable, nor do we expect you to be."

"Have you fed the dogs?", "Do you have your homework?", "Did you brush your teeth?" are often the first words out of a parent's mouth who identifies with the "to do lister" parenting approach. To enhance intention in these moments, we encourage parents to consider the idea of a threshold practice, which simply is the act of setting an intention about how you want to show up before crossing the threshold from one room into another. It is a physical signpost that you set up as a reminder that you want to be intentional.

Reshape Your Intention: Lora's experience.

Lora, a single mother of two teenage boys, examined the tension in her relationship with her boys. With so much to juggle, she felt that she was a taskmaster who rarely got time to connect with her boys in a lighter way and the boys were getting into habits of eye rolls and sarcasm that were provoking. Lora was encouraged to find her threshold practice by identifying what she wanted to remind herself of before she left her room in the morning and engaged with her boys.

Prior to leaving her room, crossing the threshold of the door, she would stand for one minute, breathing deeply in and out, with the internal mantra, "shut up and love." She would say this over and over for the full minute to remember that the to-do list was not more important than taking the time to just connect. She changed her style of connection so her first priority was hanging out, making breakfast, and having some laughter. Then, rather than dictating the to-do list to the kids, she learned to say, "keep your to-do list in mind this morning," and asked if she could help in any way. Lora witnessed a change in her tone and the boys responded in kind, though there were still a few developmentally-appropriate eye rolls.

Having a restorative practice in your day is a must when so much of your time as a parent is spent giving, doing, and perhaps self-depleting. Setting daily intentions allows you to operate with greater focus on what is important to you, moving you towards your goals rather than distracting from them.

It's common for parents to fall into the same distracting habits that their kids do and, most often, the ones that concern us the most like being plugged into a device or using substances. While plugging into a device might feel like relaxing, brainless activity, the amount of the stimulation your brain is actually receiving proves not to be restorative and, like our kids, plugging in can also cause you to shut everything else out, including your healthy intentions. It might seem like a nice distraction, but your brain needs a more soothing reprieve. Sitting with a book, writing in a journal, stretching, staring out the window for five minutes to just notice the world, especially if you have any nature within your view, is all more restorative.

 **Nugget of Knowledge:** It's difficult to create effective change if we don't know exactly what we need to change. We encourage you to take a week to pay attention to how you spend your time.

It is additionally important to understand the distinction between healthy solitude and unhealthy isolation. Healthy solitude is proactive, healing, corrective, and intentional while unhealthy isolation is reactive, depleting, and an avoidance tactic. You might be clear about what your child's isolation looks like – typically identified by the moments you want to throw the gaming console into the street – but are you also clear about your own? What do you tend to avoid and how do you avoid it? Do you get caught up in the culture of busyness and stay at work longer than you need to, or even take on work that necessitates more time at the office? Do you allow yourself to get sucked into your inbox, social media, and the never ending feeds of the internet?

Our avoidance and distraction tendencies can greatly affect our relationships and are a significant contributing factor in the health of the home. It's imperative that you take time to notice what you are distracting yourself from. Paulo Coelho, best known for his written work, "The Alchemist," says, "mistakes repeated more than once are a decision". What are the decisions you need to make, the threshold practices you want to incorporate and what do you need, from yourself or others, to be able to connect more and move more intentionally through your day?

Exercise

Distracting ways I take a break (which are ok to use in moderation).	Restorative break to incorporate.
Facebook scrolling	*5 minutes sitting outside in quiet reflection*

Your turn...

Having thoughtful intentions and threshold practices, like Lora's, are small changes that contribute to a healthier rhythm. The moment to pause before walking into a new room, in and of itself, can help you with a better routine. It is also important to remember when you create your personal rhythm and routine, you will constantly need to assess and reset. Similar to the "let's keep trying" attitude, you will build rhythms that will at times fall apart and you will have to commit to repeatedly assess and reset.

It is crucial in this process of **mastering** your intentions and **owning** your distractions that you fervently **own** your substance use. As adults face the stress of holding a home together through the expected and unexpected challenges, with a socially acceptable vice such as alcohol, it can be easy to slip into the pattern of drinking to escape. We work with parents who use marijuana as well and we hear the same reasoning from some of them that we do from their children. We work with parents who use substances with healthy balance and some who overuse and abuse. Examine this with raw honesty and, if you use and don't think you are dependent on the habit of it, whether it is alcohol or marijuana, consider the exercise of not using for one month to see what changes. As you examine your healthy rhythms, make sure that you notice why, when, and how often you turn to substances for your own relief or escape.

Budget Your Emotional Currency

Emotional currency is a way to look at how much output you can muster in a day. In interactions, there is often, if not always, an underlying emotional exchange taking place that can be identified as emotional currency being passed between us. We also spend currency on our daily decisions, when we are in traffic for example, and in each little way that our stress, anxiety, or frustration is stirred. We each have a finite amount before the coffers run dry, which is typically when we react in ways we aren't proud of, and it is important that we develop awareness over how, why, and when we spend it. This requires implementing the guiding principles of buying yourself time, critical thinking, and intention. Guide yourself by identifying and answering: what is truly worth your time and energy and why? There will of course be things that are not worth your time but that you have to give time to regardless.

Master awareness over moments when you have choice and **own** the times when you allow a situation to steal your currency, when you could have retained it. The loudness of our inner critic, ruminating thoughts, and attempts at controlling an outcome that we have no control over are a few examples of when we allow our emotional currency to be expended. Often, we spend emotional currency in many un-necessary situations. Say you, or your co-parent, forgot to get milk on the grocery run. You can spend five minutes in frustration, with yourself and with each other, or see it as a solvable problem that isn't worth spending the emotional currency on. The problem is solved by running back out to the store or by deciding that you don't need it today and you can make time to go back tomorrow. Consider which solution preserves more of your currency and go with it.

By not spending currency in the truly unnecessary moments – not crying over spilled (or forgotten) milk, as it were — you save it for the moments that will truly require it. Get into the habit of asking yourself: *Is this worth my emotional currency? Is this worth me depleting my partner's or my kid's emotional currency?* It is your responsibility to know when you are, perhaps, unnecessarily draining your emotional currency or the currency of others. **Own** it. Interacting with more intention can allow you to be thoughtful about filling your and others' buckets, rather than depleting them.

Spending Wisely: José's experience.

José talked about the dynamic in his family growing up. The buck stopped with his father and there was no confusion.

"It was different then, I guess; when my parents, especially my dad, came home and we hadn't gotten a chore done or were avoiding our homework, we knew that we would be in *big* trouble. Arguing with my parents, skipping school, these were not options in my home. We stayed on track even if we didn't like what they said or made us do. And now, our kids put their earbuds in and practically ignore us at every impasse. They have no respect for our authority the way that we had for our parents. How do I get them to know that the buck stops with me?"

This is a common theme that we see in parents who spend their emotional currency wrestling with their own upbringing, where the parents ruled, and kids obeyed (or at least were more skilled at getting away with things). Their desire was to have their children follow suit in response to the same attempt at upbringing. Kids are their own people with their own personalities and all kids and family systems are unique. It may be simply explained by the concept that what works in one family doesn't mean it will work in another, even with the best intentions. Following one ideal in parenting will almost guarantee a depletion of your emotional currency. The ability to assess and adapt your parenting style to what works for your family's uniqueness is key.

In our coaching work with José, we reshaped the idea of being powerful. Instead of needing to feel like a powerful authority over his kids, now power lies in the ability to be authentic, relational, and consistent. This included the ability to be vulnerable with open sharing in age-appropriate ways with his kids. José worked to find the balance between connecting with his kids and communicating a clear line that would have consequences if it was crossed.

José noticed that he got better responses when, instead of shouting up the stairs at his kids to do something, he would go upstairs, ask his kids to take their earbuds out for one minute so he knew they could hear him before he asked them his question. For example, "What is one responsibility you think I want you to get done now that you are home from school? What will be the consequence if it is not done?" José reported that just by changing how he interacted, both with his physical presence and willingness to give direction (not orders), he experienced preserving both his own and his kids' emotional currency, and that overall, he felt better about how he was showing up.

Lastly, to help you **master** your emotional currency, let's focus on the concept of controlling the one thing you can control: the meaning that you place on things. Placing meaning on any one event or incident can put you on a roller coaster from moment to moment. Similarly, in day-to-day life, whether at home or at work, there are moments on which we place meaning, but they might be just that, a moment. If you can see each moment as a puzzle piece and you can buy yourself time to see how additional puzzle pieces come together, your roller coaster might become more of a lazy river, or something in between the two.

Managing Your Currency: Beth's experience.

Following a phone call with her son in treatment, Beth reached out to discuss the "terrible" call. Her 13-year-old son had just received her letter that explained that he would transition from wilderness therapy to a therapeutic boarding school and the phone call was the next day. She shared about his anger, his bargaining, his claiming that he had learned all that he needed to learn, and he struggled to shift from the topic and from the intensity of his emotion about it.

"I was so disappointed," she shared. As we explored why, she explained that she had hoped for more, to discuss other things, and for him to be able to manage his emotions a bit better. She also stated that her next few days were challenging as she was overwhelmed with sadness and struggled to move through her days in the ways she would have liked.

Throughout our time together, Beth identified the roller coaster she would be on, joining in whatever emotion her son was expressing and depleting her emotional currency in her day-to-day life as a result. With this situation, we used the puzzle piece analogy to address the importance of not placing meaning on the situation just yet, slowing down the roller coaster effect a bit. We encouraged her to wait to place meaning until more time had passed and helped her to understand there were other puzzle pieces to consider. These included her response to him, his work with his peers, therapist, and field staff in the days to follow, the letter he would write next, and their next phone call.

His initial reaction, we explained, was pretty healthy and age-appropriate and represented the start of a grief cycle for him. His next letter and their next phone call a week later illustrated his ability to put new skills into action and he even asked her to hold him accountable for not arguing on their next call. The interactions were healthier, he was able to focus on other topics while still expressing his honest emotion about the transition and shifted his focus to identifying the items he might need before the transition to his new school. Taking the time to allow more pieces to come together before meaning is placed on a moment is a great way to **master** emotional currency.

Master Healthy Practices

The body stores emotion, including those little "t" traumas in which impact can often be minimized. Our body, mind, and experiences are interwoven which really means, we think we are skilled at discounting the impact of those traumas, but our body often tells us otherwise. Emotions are felt and expressed within the body, often confined as we actively deal with the difficult situation at hand, move on, and don't realize the emotions stop moving through us and end up accumulating in different parts of the body, sometimes bringing on physical discomfort or illness.

Your body needs your attention. It needs a breathing practice to soothe the overactive mind and quiet the heightened release of stress hormones. It needs the right food to fuel it, it needs a rhythm of movement or exercise to keep it going. Your body needs you to be connected and aware, to listen to it, and support it. Creating a rhythm and routine that focuses on your body in an active way through intentional breathing and movement, allows you the space and opportunity to increase your emotional awareness and management.

While working on developing a routine with a recent client whose son is in a wilderness therapy program, she said, "It is amazing how a little repetition helps me follow through and it feels so good! I have been going on a daily bike ride with music playing on an MP3, so I don't have to bring my phone, and it sets me up well for the ups and downs that might come through the day." The importance of body first, mind second when starting off the day, allows for the mind to then perform and respond intellectually instead of emotionally when issues arise.

We encourage you to commit to a routine and find your rhythm with intentional movement. For some, this will look like a clear exercise routine and for others it will look like just finding moments of sustained movement in the day. Finding your rhythm, the one that fits you, will make it easier to get started and to stay with it. And, when you fall out of the habit, that is ok. Be gentle with yourself. Notice that you fell out of it and restart it. Again and again and again.

Restoring and **mastering** healthy practices often takes all of our senses. It can be helpful to utilize a simple "sensory treasure hunt" next time you are out on a walk or a run. Notice a few things you hear, see, smell, touch, and even taste. Keep the focus for a period of time within each sense being used. Another option is to have a mindfulness practice in which you practice noticing details. For example, picking up a leaf or stone and really looking at it, noticing all the details you can. Consider taking some time to write about your experience and whether you allowed yourself to take the opportunity to be more awe-inspired by taking notice in a different way.

Your personal rhythms as well as those you set up with your family, such as a weekly family meeting or family walk in the park, will ebb and flow. Some, you will learn do not fit your family or your schedules and it is important to remember the intention, assess the needs, adjust, and rebuild as necessary. Just like with any New Year's resolution, you will follow through for a time, then fall out of the habit. With awareness and intention, you can rebuild and reset rather than allowing it all to fall to the wayside without picking it back up. This is natural and normal for everyone, including your child who will have their own ebb and flow when it comes to commitment and follow through.

As we support your development of a restorative rhythm and routine, you likely have a list you have considered in the past and ideas you would like to pursue moving forward. This is an opportunity for you to **own** and **master** your intentional plan that supports the mind and the body as you go through this experience. While you have a child in treatment, it is a great time to implement your daily or weekly routine, establish the routines of your household and how responsibilities are shared, in order to shape it all with more intention.

Remember. Reflect. Revisit.

- **Own** and **master** the sacred pause – Sacred because it is time that is clearly dedicated to a higher purpose, looking deep within, to discover who you really are and where you want to be. When we are forced to pause in our life, reflection can occur and the opportunity to implement change follows.
- Discover healthy rhythms, even small ones, that can replenish you and be honest about the reasons you use to avoid making a change.
- **Master** slowing down as much as you can, even just for moments, to have time for thoughtful intentions about how you want to show up during a certain situation or interaction.

- Emotional currency is real; be clear on how, why, and when you spend it and do it with more attention and awareness.

Chapter 8

The Invitation To Change & Redefine Your Values

Master Your Values: Paul, Annie, & Kate's experience.

While working with Paul, Annie, and Kate, the dad, stepmom, and mom of Dawn, their 15-year-old daughter in wilderness therapy, we started a discussion about values early on in the process. As a blended family, they had taken the time and worked together to define what values were most important to them to guide the process of shaping their family as whole, even though it was split into two separate households. "Openness, education, kindness toward others, balance between responsibility and play, being in service to others, and communication," were all at the top of the list.

"Prior to sending Dawn to wilderness therapy, we weren't aware of how far off track we had gotten," Paul shared. Like many parents, the issues are recognizable but difficult to see when in the thick of it.

To help them with a much-needed reset, as an exercise, we encouraged them to make a list of their values and a list of what they called, "the Dark Side values". When they revisited the norm they had fallen into prior to treatment and examined what home looked like, they decided that it was the Dark Side values that were in charge. We went through an activity of raw honesty, in which they came up with farcical values that seemed to have taken over, such as, "we value education unless Dawn has a stomachache and doesn't want to go to school," and, "we only encourage balanced living if it includes something Dawn wants to do."

Collectively, we were able to laugh about some of the things they came up with such as, our favorites: "have a healthy relationship with technology unless Dawn makes a solid, 'but everyone is doing it' argument," and, "even though we are more experienced, fully formed, high-functioning adults, it is important to let Dawn make all of the decisions about how we live our lives." By recognizing how their values became skewed and taking the time to redefine their values, they were able to have a chance for a family reset and this shaped much of their letter-writing communication with Dawn.

Paul, Annie, and Kate are like many families who are in need of a reset, which is challenging when the pace of the day is so quick and it seems like you are moving from crisis to crisis. And so now is the time, here in this sacred pause you are encouraged to take, to dig deep and do a personal reset. Taking the time to identify the most important values to you, and why they are important, can guide you as you shape your rules and the guardrails you set up at home to help keep things on track. Look at what your Dark Side values were with some raw honesty and feel free to laugh a bit at some of the ridiculousness of it all. Yes, at times it is heartbreaking to see where things got to in the past and utilizing some humor as you look in the mirror can bring important levity.

As you redefine your values, which we encourage you to not wait on, look at how you are living true to them right now, today, and what you can change about your daily rhythm, especially if you still have children at home, to guide things with them in mind. If service work is important to you for example, ask yourself if you are engaging in it yourself and, if not, how do you want to bring it back into your life?

Exercise

Redefining values:

Dark Side values that had taken over	Values that you want steering the ship
Turn a blind eye to tech overuse	*Commit to healthy balanced use for everyone and the guardrails that you might have to be in charge of to enforce balance*

Your turn...

Own Your Authentic Renewal

The power of change requires the willingness to dig deep, to decide that the changes you want to make will authentically come from within and that you truly value those desired changes for yourself. That sort of authentic renewal is more likely to lead to long term success. However, to invest in authentic renewal, you have to find within yourself the power of change which orders you to understand the internal obstacles to self-change, change you want to make in relation-ships, change you want to make as a parent. If we don't identify those obstacles, they will continue to rear their ugly heads and stand in the way of your desired change, no matter how committed you are.

Katy Milkman, who has a degree in Engineering as well as a doctorate in Computer Science and Business, wrote a fabulous book on change: "How to Change, The Science of Getting from Where You Are to Where You Want to Be". Her book provides extraordinary research and guidance when it comes to a person's ability to engage in and have true transformational change. In addition to our encouragement to read her book, hold on to the wisdom she shares as you are identifying your internal obstacles and investing in your authentic renewal.

Katy suggests, "Your opponent is inside your head. Maybe it's forgetful-ness, or a lack of confidence, or laziness or the tendency to succumb to temptation. Whatever the challenge, the best tacticians size up their opponent and play accordingly." As you absorb the many tools that can contribute to a healthier lifestyle for your child in treatment and consider these tools as options for your family, you will have to invest in the process of authentic renewal to be successful at implementing these tools in your home.

We hear from many parents who plan to put changes into place once their child comes home. "Once our child comes home, how can we put new technology rules into place with everyone and shift our rhythm?" Here is *our* question: If you see these new tools and restorative rhythms as important, why would you wait? There are communication skills that can benefit all of your relationships – with family, friends, and even at work. There are restorative rhythms that can benefit your life *and* can help you to move up on the "great role model" scale. If you have kids at home who can benefit from what you are learning, whether it is a weekly family meeting or screen time rules, make the changes now.

You are fortifying your home, your rhythms, your rules to make home a healthy place now and to ensure a solid foundation for everyone. And be cautious that you don't blame the child in treatment for the changes you decide on. Instead of saying, "we are doing this because it will be important for your brother when he gets home and his therapist is suggesting it," say, "we are learning about things that are important to us that we want to change." Claim it, **own** it. Period. These are the opportunities for you to claim and **own** your parenting decisions. It will be very difficult to make sustainable changes if you don't **own** them as yours.

Exercise

Identify what your internal obstacles are that stand between you and the personal and parenting success you are wanting to achieve. Establish a game plan to meet *your* opponent.

Identifying what is your opponent (the obstacle)	Strategies for winning (action steps you will utilize)	What changes about your life will occur if you do it
The need to be right	*Listen more, argue less, stop keeping score and correcting*	*Others will see me as a safe person to be right and wrong in front of– decrease tension in home*

Your turn…

Radical Acceptance

Radical acceptance refers to the act of letting go of the need to control a situation and accepting the situation for what it is. This does not mean you are complacent, but rather you are intentional with focusing on what you have control over in a situation without battling, internally or externally, with the things over which you don't have control.

To radically accept a situation, you identify what the distressing moment was, what you did or others did to contribute to the moment and what control you have right now to manage it in a solutions focused way. To not accept a situation for what it was, battling it, and wishing it was different, is to give away your emotional currency, at times unnecessarily. When we coach radical acceptance with parents, we often refer to the difference between pain and suffering. Pain, in the Buddhist allegories, is referred to as being shot by an arrow. There is a physical sensation and an emotional one that comes along with it. Suffering is like being shot with a second arrow and it is the resistance to that pain and the battle against it that increases the suffering and again strips our emotional currency.

Why the focus on radical acceptance, pain, and suffering? We often find that the challenges that lead a family to seek out wilderness therapy are the first arrow; the grief about the situation and the shame many parents feel hit like the second arrow. We see parents depleting themselves as they try to hide from their community; relationships take a major hit as parents get stuck in shaming and blaming each other for the situation they are in, which is a distraction from **owning** the role you play in moving forward and **mastering** the skills you can build to get there. Unfortunately, we see kids who come home from treatment exploit that shame to get back on an unhealthy path. This alone could give you reason to invest in radical acceptance.

How we accept our pain is a question that often surfaces in the parents we support. How do we let go of the responses that are not serving us and reduce our suffering when what we are dealing with is so difficult? Learning to sit in your discomfort is the foundation of all your work and it's one of the hardest practices you will be asked to do: knowing your discomfort is real and it's not going anywhere anytime soon, and learning how to find comfort while you sit in the discomfort nonetheless.

Master Vulnerability: Mike's experience.

Mike was the father of an 18-year-old in treatment and he was preparing to go see his son for a family visit. We helped Mike prepare for what to expect and encouraged him to show up with the skills in mind he had been **honing**, including ways to practice vulnerability and sit in his discomfort. For Mike, and for many parents who tend to skirt the surface of their emotions, vulnerability included sitting in his discomfort without trying to distract from it, change or fix it.

"This whole vulnerability concept is like running down main street naked," Mike mused aloud. "I think I'd rather do that." Like many parents who take this opportunity, upon returning from the visit, Mike shared, "It was the longest, most connected conversation I have had with my son in the last two years, even when the topics were difficult."

Personally and professionally, it is not lost on us as to how difficult this task is. What we will continue to remind you is that we do not become resilient human beings by having pleasurable and easy experiences, we establish and build resilience by experiencing and navigating our most difficult emotions and discomforts.

Finding that comfort comes through increasing your self-awareness and vulnerability, and being open to the feedback you are receiving about your child, yourself, and your family system. Sitting with the discomfort can be supported by, for example, focusing on whole truths such as claiming that perhaps the entire sky isn't falling, even if parts of it are.

Know that if you truly accept the discomfort and put into practice what you can control, like implementing daily habits and changes that will serve you in a positive way, you will start to experience finding comfort while you sit in the current discomfort. This practice will also remind you it's important for everyone, including, actually *especially*, your children to learn how to sit in their discomfort and learn how to navigate difficult emotions. This will be their greatest skill in building and increasing resiliency – simply, the ability to bounce back when life throws curve balls.

Finding Your People

To feel the sense of belonging that comes when you have found your people is to know what it means to be held with love and truly accepted on your best days and your worst. Acceptance is one of our basic needs as humans and if you have not already, this is an ideal time to find those people who accept you just for being yourself and all that comes with you, especially in this difficult time for you and your family.

One of the emotions that acts as an obstacle to acceptance and to finding your people is shame. Shame is a painful feeling of humiliation or distress caused by the consciousness of wrong or foolish behavior. In your role as a parent, ask yourself: what have you done that is foolish, in seeking alternative support for your struggling child? If he needed help in an academic area that you were not proficient in, would you feel ashamed that you had to outsource support due to your lack of knowledge?

Of course, this type of situation has less stigma but the question we ask ourselves over and over is: *why are parents expected to be the experts and manage it all at home when it comes to mental, social, emotional, and behavioral challenges?* Many of you tried several options at home before deciding that there were too many obstacles blocking your child's ability to thrive. Where is the shame in that? Many parents express shame about not having been "enough" for their children, for contributing to the problems, for not noticing something soon enough.

The reality is that we are not enough on our own. How long has it been said that "it takes a village"? Even those of us who are highly trained can be too wrapped up in the emotion of the day-to-day to see all the signs and even with training, how we contribute to the challenges in our home. We are human, not perfect family-rearing robots.

Radically accepting the challenges you and your family have faced can help you connect to a community and find your people. Having a community of people who know your story, who want to hear about it to support you, who are open to talking about it, and open to not talking about it depending on your needs, is key.

Shame can keep us isolated. A person or a family needing mental health care, which sadly continues to have a shaming stigma in our society – though significantly less so than even 15 years ago – can still cause parents to remain isolated. The number of parents we work with who believe they are the only ones in their town with this story is surprising to us. We find that, when we encourage parents to find their people with authenticity about their story, others will share something similar and then community is built. Those parents also believed they were the only ones and so you have the opportunity to start a revolution of support simply by taking the risk of vulnerability and being open enough to share.

This is also an area to ask yourselves what you are modeling. While you might need to be discerning rather than singing your story from the rooftops it is important that your child who is in treatment doesn't experience you as being ashamed of them.

Eventually, when your child is home, they will need to find *their* people and you will not be able to control what story they share about the experience. There will be some friends who hear only the "war stories" of the experience and other friends who hear the more tender pieces. There will be conversations you overhear that you will want to interject in or afterward where you might want to ask, "but what about all of the good stuff you gained from the experience?"

This can be experienced by parents as uncontrollable exposure and the discomfort of that can be palpable. Strength-ening your resolve with clarity for yourselves about your own story can help you to be a more solid vessel for the stories your child chooses to share. It is important that you do not try to control the story that your child shares, as this story will develop for them over the years and your attempt to force the positive spin will feel invalidating and could cause them to hold on even tighter to the not-so-pleasant aspect of the experience.

Shame is an emotion we all experience, one that brings a significant amount of discomfort and is extremely difficult to sit in. The experience of feeling shame shapes our interactions and depending on how we navigate it, will affect how we show up in those interactions. Brené Brown, PhD, has invested her career in commanding those who are interested in this type of deep work to deal with their shame and its negative impact on their lives, hence why we use her words to describe the management of shame:

"Shame needs three things to grow exponentially: secrecy, silence, and judgment. Those are not authentic responses. So, dealing with shame while maintaining authenticity and cultivating more courage, connection, and compassion in your relationships is what's needed. It's a tall order. But one of the byproducts of being able to move through shame constructively is that people who come out the other side by default feel braver, more connected, and compassionate."

Own Your Communication

In Part 1 we focused on learning and **honing** your communication and in Part 3, we will focus on **mastering** and **enacting** new skills for when you bring your child home from treatment by sharing communication tips that can help to shape the tone of the relationship with your child. In this part, right now, we need to focus on you and the importance of **owning** your communication.

We have been on phone and video calls with parents since we began as wilderness therapists decades ago. Well, video calls came much later. In these parenting calls, it can become clear very quickly who takes the verbal lead and who tends to be more in the shadows. On these calls, we also glean an individual's learning style; some parents need to hear things more concretely and get specific guidance around the what and the how of a topic and some respond better to a more relational approach.

We support parents as they get to know their comm-unication style and how they process information – some of us are slower, some faster with how information soaks in. We have parents who quietly listen and chew on information before responding and we have parents who interrupt others impulsively, worried that if they don't, they will forget the piece they wanted to contribute.

- What is your honest self-assessment, which might include feedback from others, about how you communicate?
- Are you aware of when you are truly listening, rather than waiting for your millisecond to be heard?
- Do you jump in to share your own similar story that someone is telling you as a way to connect?
- Do you take the talking lead?
- Are you aggressive when disagreeing with someone?
- Are you more passive, holding back your thoughts on something?
- Do you need time to process something before responding to it in a wise-minded way?
- How do you communicate when you are right? Or when you are wrong?
- How do you respond when you receive feedback?

This last piece is an important one to understand since your child is in the midst of **mastering** both giving and receiving feedback daily; many parents express frustration when their children are defensive, at which point we typically ask parents how they respond in similar situations. The response is typically accompanied by an audible gulp.

Let's give the word "trigger" a moment here. While this has become a commonly used term, in the treatment world, for many parents it is new to their day-to-day vocabulary. To "be triggered" suggests that one has an emotion that elicits reactivity. "Triggered" is then used as shorthand in the treatment world to cover an array of experiences. As coaches, we have found that people use it and unknowingly deflect from further exploration of underlying emotions. When the word is presented to you in a conversation, use it as an opportunity to gather more information about what is being conveyed to you and to explore further.

As you delve into your personal growth and get to know more about your communication, reactions, and responses, it is of the utmost importance to understand your triggers and, if possible, from where they developed. Intimately understanding these pieces of how you work can help build awareness and slow reaction time to those triggers. Are you triggered by tone, by being interrupted, by someone texting while you are talking? Are you triggered simply when someone disagrees with your perspective or when someone is drunk?

These triggers might not change for you and you might always have an internal reaction. Your job, for yourself and for your family, is to be aware. Knowing is half the battle, as they say. It is the easy half but if you are at least aware of the trigger, you might be able to buy yourself time for long enough to notice and change your reaction. Even if you react in a way you wish you had not, if you are aware and **own** your part in things, you can reach out to repair after a reaction.

Slowing Down to Master Reactions: Sara's experience.

Sara, a parent preparing to bring her child home from wilderness therapy, to illustrate her awareness and growth, shared with us a story about an interaction with her neighbor.

"We previously had not seen eye to eye on a situation and she, in an email that went out to several parents at our school, without naming me, said that her entitled neighbor was an example of the entitlement within the school." Sara went on to explain that her initial internal reaction was a defensive one and that she wanted to "reply all" with her side of the story, as everyone knew they were neighbors. "But since we had been focusing so much on awareness of triggers and slowing my reaction time, I stopped and walked away."

Sara sat with her journal to answer questions we had highlighted as important awareness-building guides for her:

- *What about this is triggering for me?*
- *Is there something in the message that is important for me to hear or consider as possibly true?*
- *What would a response look like that ensures I show up as my best self?*

These were the questions we developed to help her filter communication from others in a wise-minded way, rather than in a defensive way. It is through identifying and committing to a process similar to this for yourself that you can disentangle from the emotional hooks that trigger reactions. And, through practicing this awareness in varying interactions, you become more of a **master** of it when the stakes are high with your child and family.

Practices such as Sara's contribute to healthy communication with others and to feeling restored rather than drained during challenging interactions. Even if a situation does not go perfectly, the ability to walk away feeling proud of how you showed up in a moment is hugely beneficial. The book "Crucial Conversations: Tools for Talking when Stakes are High" is a great place to go after reading this, if learning to communicate when emotionally triggered is at the top of your list. **Owning** and **mastering** habits such as these further helps you shape the tone of your home through improving communication with the co-parenting team. The more wise-minded and intentionally thoughtful you are, the more responsive and less reactive you will be.

Exercise

Take time to identify your triggers and new possible responses to practice.

Trigger	Why does it trigger me?	My negative reactions to it.	How would I prefer to react?
Being interrupted	Not feeling heard as a child	Shutting down and isolating	Change the meaning I place on it and ask for what I need

Your turn…

Master Co-parenting Communication

In an intact family, one of the ultimate goals in a co-parenting relationship is to communicate in a way that illustrates that you truly value the other person. You are in the trenches together and when in a battle zone, you need each other to survive and thrive. You need to believe that the other person is worthy and valuable, and you need to role model that to your kids. This is never more difficult than when you have a child battling mental, emotional, social, or cognitive challenges and when the intensity of the situation in front of you is at its most critical. While you might see things differently, it is unlikely that one of you is always right all of the time.

Whether you're intact, split, or blended, in general when working with a co-parenting team, we typically aim to get everyone into a shared agreement that somewhere in be-tween each version of a story is the actual truth. You have biases, emotions, history, and baggage through which most of your experiences are filtered. It is rare to have two people witness the same situation and leave with the same story. As such, if you can agree that somewhere in the middle is a truth, then you can also agree that the solution to a problem is somewhere in between what each side believes it to be.

Further, if you can practice validating the message that someone is trying to convey without being on a quest for the exact truth of a story, you can build bridges and enhance your relationships. Keep in mind through our teaching, we're working toward the idea of "good enough" communication. The goal is not to be a perfect robot with skillful responses to *every* interaction. Keep practicing to build "good enough" **mastery** so that you can **enact** new skills at least some of the time.

Here is a sample of a not-so-good exchange:

> Parent 1: "You always are dismissive of my parenting line, and you aren't even here all day to know why I am saying what I am saying, and you did it again when I told Morgan she couldn't drive the car for the next few days and you said, 'well, let's just wait to decide on that, maybe she can.' Sometimes you need to stay out of it because you are such a pushover!"

> Parent 2: "Well you are always throwing out consequences unnecessarily and without even talking to me and I was not in agreement with taking away her driving privileges because then I have to get her to school in the morning and she is *never* on time."

And a good enough version that **enacts** some of our guidance:

Parent 1: "I felt dismissed when I told Morgan she couldn't drive the car for the next few days and you said 'well, let's just wait to decide on that, maybe she can.' I'd like to share with you what led into that and see if you can back me on it or if we can come up with something we both agree on."

Parent 2: "I can see how it came across as dismissive. I could have asked you, not in front of Morgan, about why that was your line before I jumped in. I was thinking that, if she pulled herself together and got homework done, actually picked up her room, and did the dishes you keep asking her to help with, that we could give her another chance. I do tend to cave more often so maybe we can talk about a middle ground for next time but let's go with what you set up this time."

Take a moment to notice the difference between the exchanges. Hear the attacking and defensive tones in the first sample; the blaming, the blanket and exaggerated "always/never" statements. In the second, you can see validation, **ownership**, "I" statements, and collaboration. When learning "good enough" communication styles, we are often quick to point out what the other person can do to improve the communication. We hope you take this opportunity to consider a few of your recent interactions and identify how you could have shown up differently, even if the other person stayed the same. **Own** it, just like you hope your child does when you point out their interactions.

Communicating in increments, in bits over a set time period, can help you to **master** the middle ground. Listen to what your co-parenting partner shares, commit to taking time to think about it, sit with it, write about it, and then agree on a time and place where you will get back together to hear the other side and offer the listener the same time to process. Working through one topic at a time can help with this, so there is not a laundry list of resentments or "should have's" that you are trying to unload.

Intact as a couple or operating only as a co-parenting team, there is always a need to cooperate and operate as effectively and efficiently as possible. Often co-parenting teams do not invest the time needed to communicate all that needs to be addressed which includes acknowledging what is interfering with the co-parenting team's success.

Collaborative Co-Parenting: Jason & Maggie's experience.

Jason and Maggie are one of many co-parenting teams, no longer a couple, that we have supported, and like all co-parenting teams, they had a lot to manage. There were issues that often interfered with their ability to show up as the united front they wanted to be. Their lack of communication to unite their decisions often led them to parent unilaterally which caused greater conflict between them.

"Our ability to see how we could work together as a co-parenting team, despite our differences, came once we acknowledged and figured out a couple of keys: the import-ance of creating time to talk about the decisions we had to make and making the effort to actually collaborate by add-ressing the issues that were interfering, such as taking things personally and shutting each other out. Then, we made deals and commitments to each other, which supported us with showing up more aligned for kids."

When a co-parenting team is successful and makes communication the priority, it comes from a shared conviction and commitment to putting the co-parenting team, or for some, the couple, first. There becomes a willingness to form agreements and make plans on how to better manage the obstacles and untangle the conflicts with grace that allows the co-parenting team to thrive.

We used to say that parenting was the hardest job on the planet, but it might be truer to say that co-parenting wins the prize for the most challenging job. Important to note is that the majority of parents we support, whether married, divorced, separated, or in a blended family, believe in the same values and want to guide their family toward the same values. They are aligned on the macro and somewhat misaligned on the micro – the ways that those values are **enacted** in the day-to-day. Luckily, you have already spent weeks, if not years, understanding the role you play, the ways you work well together and the ways that you work against each other, and you have new skills, habits, and communication strategies to put into place so that you don't fall into familiar old patterns.

One big test of this might be in making the decision about the next step for your child who is in treatment. Your challenge is to **enact** some of the habits you have learned for finding a middle ground when you see things differently. As you face this decision, we recommend that parents identify the emotional and the practical pros and cons of your options *and* that you work to have as many pros as you do cons to each option, in order to push yourselves to truly be critical thinkers. Additionally, wait until you are given specific placement options to review this so that you have details rather than simply comparing the concepts of "home" and "away."

Exercise

Home

Emotional Pros:	Practical Pros:
Time together	*Financial ease*

Your turn...

Emotional Cons:	Practical Cons:
Increased tension	*Access to drugs*

Your turn...

Specific Therapeutic Placement

Emotional Pros:	Practical Pros:
Potential for enhanced relationship through skill building	*All support built in*

Your turn...

Emotional Cons:	Practical Cons:
Fear she will see it as punishment	*Flights to go see her and work schedules*

Your turn...

In contentious relationships, with both our therapist and parent coach hats on, we have gone so far as to ask parents to step into their children's shoes and answer, "20 years from now, looking back, how will they describe what they witnessed in their parents?" They are always watching and are more aware than we know. Will it be that what they witnessed were parents who kept each other in court for as long as possible to ensure each other's misery or that you were not able to move on in your own life and remained consumed with the life of your ex? Will it be that you had major differences but found a way to work through it as best as you could? This is harsh and direct, we know. And it is extremely important.

A recent client, when told we were working on this book and when asked what she wished she knew or was told when her child went through treatment said, "I wish they had been more direct. I wish they were not as worried about our feelings and that they could have just come out and said that my ex and I were doing a terrible job. But no one was willing to be that clear and that direct, and we figured it out too late."

So, for parents, whether married, separated, or divorced, remember that no matter where you are in your personal relationship, you are expected to show up and find your way to effectively co-parent together. **Own** your part in this, **master** a wise-minded approach, be more thoughtful about your emotional currency, radically accept that you cannot control what others do, and captain your ship with more grace... make *that* your legacy and remind yourself you can be the adult you hope your children grow to become.

Our go-to guiding principle, curiosity, can help with this, as can responding in more wise-minded ways. The main goal of being aware of emotional currency, how you deplete it and how you restore it, is to cause less harm to yourself and others. Your ability to do this will also depend on your ability to recognize the underlying emotional currency exchanged and your willingness to recognize your emotional experience in the moment.

Reshaping Your Role Through Communication

Couples' therapists John and Julie Gottman studied over 4,000 couples and identified key factors that contributed to the couples who had more success in their marriages. Not so surprisingly, communication skills were a key factor, especially in relation to managing conflict. The Gottmans introduced the theory of the Four Horsemen of the Apocalypse, as well as provided us with the antidote. Their concepts work for healthy communication with all relationships, intact or not. Many treatment programs teach The Four Horsemen Theory as it resembles many of the tools they teach surrounding communication.

The four communication approaches to avoid are criticism, contempt, defensiveness, and stonewalling, the ones they predicted would end a relationship if continued. The antidotes are similar to the new teaching strategies you are hearing that your child is learning as he navigates his current "family", his peer group, and the staff members he lives with each rotating week.

Find how to express a complaint without expressing *criticism*, which includes deploying the antidote of using a soft start-up as you enter a conversation using "I" statements to communicate. Building a culture of appreciation and respect, as an antidote, decreases the tendency to communicate in passive aggressive ways, increasing *contempt*, which assumes a position of moral superiority in the relationship. Taking responsibility and **ownership** of your choices, will help decrease the *defensiveness* in the relationship. This is a great antidote to look for in your child during the treatment process. The more responsible they are, the more **ownership** and accountability they are willing to take, the more authentic they are in their change. Taking time to self-soothe, increasing calmness, creates a great antidote to *stonewalling*, a form of conflict avoidance that decreases the ability to manage the challenges.

All varieties of co-parenting teams are well served by implementing these types of theories to help create more functional, healthy, and positive approaches to enhance the co-parenting relationship. Personality differences will continue to impact all couples and co-parenting teams alike, however, addressing and **owning** the obstacles and problems, in-creasing effective communication skills, and utilizing the tools taught to you, will help you to achieve the co-parenting success needed.

You likely have had some education on the drama triangle, also known as the "dreaded drama triangle" originally developed by Stephen Karpman and later reshaped by others. The drama triangle identifies common roles we play in communication and labels those roles as "victim", "persecutor", and "rescuer". The theory is that, in a triad, (two parents and a child, let's say), someone tends to be the victim and the other two roles contribute to that person being in the victim role through the roles they take on.

The roles we play are born somewhat out of our natural tendencies and somewhat out of the position we tend to hold in the family, often one we take on due to the *perceived* effectiveness of the role. The person more in charge of accountability and follow through tends to take on the "persecutor" position, for example. In order to move out of the unhealthy roles that we take on, we have to start with believing that the one who is typically the "victim" is actually capable.

To overcome the unhealthy patterns in the drama triangle while still acknowledging the important role in the dynamic, David Emerald identifies more empowering roles for each person to take on in The Empowerment Dynamic, because truly, who wants to raise their hand for any of the roles in the drama triangle? This dynamic teaches how to rethink the roles that are played and to choose more empowering roles one can incorporate in themselves as well as within their relationships. In this new triangle, the role of the persecutor becomes the challenger and the role of the rescuer shifts to the coach which ultimately allows the victim to become their own creator, helping them see their competencies and the power they have over how their life moves. In order to make important changes in your family dynamic, this model can help you to **own** and **master** the healthy version of the role you play.

Reshaping Your Role: Paul & Annie's experience.

The drama triangle work was integral for Paul and Annie as they explored the dynamics of their home and the triad with Dawn.

"There were times when I was in the process of holding a screen time limit with Dawn and she would start to escalate. Annie, just home from work and not wanting to come home to an argument, would come in the room and offer to extend the screen time limit without even gathering information before interjecting," reported Paul. Paul went on to share that he would leave the room feeling like the rug was pulled out from under him after parenting on his own through the day and that, "Annie would get to be the good guy again just to avoid conflict."

As we spoke about the intention behind each of their positions in this situation and worked to have a process of slowing down to first understand where they were each coming from, we identified how they could shift to the "challenger" and the "coach." If Annie came home to a similar situation in the future, her job as the coach would be to support the interaction by encouraging Dawn to find healthy ways to communicate her frustrations. As the coach, Annie also keeps herself from getting into the middle. Paul, in the challenger role, developed language that was more supportive while still holding the line, which made Annie feel more comfortable and less likely to unnecessarily intervene.

There is so much to teach surrounding this empowering approach to navigating family triads with the most noticeable aspect being that it is simply empowering for parents. It is strength-based parenting that allows a parent to single-handedly be in the role of the coach and then jump to the role of a challenger in one conversation. It also allows a co-parenting team to have easy awareness of the role their co-parent is taking on in the conversation with their child and to assess if they want to join them in perhaps challenging as well or maybe coaching because the challenging role is being positively utilized. In the end, in both roles, no matter who plays them, the ultimate goal and hopeful result is a child learning to become their own creator making and **owning** choices for themselves.

As you work to understand the drama triangle and the importance of shifting roles, such as rescuing, to effect change in the family, it is equally imperative to understand and avoid rescue trauma. We coined the phrase rescue trauma, or at least we think we coined it, in reference to the uncertainty about whether you are being a loving parent or rescuing your child unnecessarily.

You will learn a lot through your child's stay in treatment about the various ways you have rescued your child and potentially impacted their ability to develop certain com-petencies due to jumping in too quickly. And you will become a bit nervous and unclear about when and if you are rescuing. This is where developing a wise-minded parenting gut can help you tremendously and where knowing the difference between incidents and patterns can help provide clarity.

We want to make this very clear – you are allowed to be a loving parent who wants to do things for your child. You are allowed to make him sandwiches and you are allowed to pick her up from school when she says she is sick. If you are *always* the only one making him a sandwich or if she needs to get picked up every day, then you are likely leaning into rescuing. Sometimes you can pull the sandwich makings out and have him make a sandwich for you and himself, sometimes you can do it together. We have actually coined this the "sandwich spectrum" (very official, we know) and as long as you are doing a little bit of each style along the spectrum, you are doing ok. And, if she is calling home every day with a stomachache, make a doctor's appointment.

Having a wise-minded parenting gut requires that you are clear about where the voice of your parenting gut is coming from. Is it urging you to make a decision out of fear of conflict? Is it driving you toward the most logical choice without considering the emotional? Is it the voice of your mother and driven by your search for her approval or the voice from the trauma of an alcoholic father? You need to develop trust in your gut, know why it is directing you in a certain way and get familiar with what it sounds like when it is in a wise-minded place. That will help you know when you are being a loving parent and when you are rescuing and thus keeping your child in the role of the victim.

Your job with the (dreaded) drama triangle is to truly understand its impact and to label the role(s) that you tend to play, whether you use the language of the drama triangle or not. Some use the language in describing the roles as good guy, bad guy, or even hero, villain, and victim. All roles need each player to take responsibility for the role they play and to do their part to help the triad get unstuck, by individually finding their way out of the dread. So, examine the intentions behind the role, how your role interacts, in healthy or unhealthy ways with the other two roles, and develop an understanding and a language set that allows you to capitalize on the strengths and intentions of the role you play.

A side note on the "good guy, bad guy" language with parenting: typically the person who is more consistent with accountability and line holding is seen as and sees themselves as the bad guy. We invite you to change the paradigm and to see that role as the superhero. While there are always aspects to **hone**, such as the tone and timing of delivery or with a threshold practice, the family needs a superhero to help keep it all on track. So, if you have seen yourself as a bad guy, you officially have permission to start wearing a cape and walking around with your fist on your hip in the classic superhero pose saying to yourself, "I am a superhero".

Chapter 9

Supporting Siblings Through the Sacred Pause

As part of this sacred pause, this pause that is dedicated to a higher purpose, it continues to be important to take time for the siblings at home. You love your children. All of them. This work that you are doing for yourself and alongside your child who is in treatment has the bonus of benefiting everyone in your family.

Supporting siblings at home when you have a child in treatment includes working in new ways through your day-to-day as well as supporting them with critical thinking, as they decide what role they want to play, or not, with their sibling in treatment. If they are unsure about writing, guide them through some pros and cons, theirs and yours, and let them know you support what they choose. If they are hanging out with friends who are asking about their sibling, which also happens with teachers, coaches, and extended family, consider formulating a response with them that fits the situation and feels right to everyone.

It's key that you not set out to control what they say but engage in a conversation about what they want to say, how saying what they want to will help them and how that fits with your family. Younger children often are less aware of the reasons why their sibling is no longer at home and often experience grief. This grief can be compounded when they are asked about their sibling by those outside the family so helping them find simple answers will help. While older siblings may have a significant amount of awareness, they too are feeling a wide range of emotions they can't quite articulate. Helping them through curious and thoughtful conversation can help them bring language to what they are feeling and thinking, making it easier to navigate those tough questions from people outside your immediate family.

Many siblings experience trauma caused by their sibling who is now in treatment, and this is not to be minimized and viewed as normal sibling conflict. This is the time for you as the parent to identify the true impact the sibling relationship has endured and what support siblings at home may need, either through conversations with you or with a professional.

Additionally, at this point in your journey, it is important to examine what is going well at home and what you are doing to help things to go well. Notice the tough moments and anything similar or different in your responses.

"You never would have said anything about that when Tyler was home," stated a 15-year-old whose brother, Tyler, was in treatment, when mom called him out for a sassy remark.

"I had to ask myself if there was any truth in it, even though I just wanted to defend myself and tell him to check himself, and he was right. Tyler took up so much of the air in the room and his challenges got all of our attention; even bold remarks from the other kids fell on deaf ears," the mom shared during a coaching session. She identified several things about the interaction she had learned from coaching that helped things go better than they might have, including slowing her reaction time, not taking the bait, validating his emotions even though she did not entirely agree with his side of the story, and dealing with the situation in increments rather than hammering through it all in one sitting.

If you learned that you tend toward the "rescuer" role, notice if and when you engage in the rescuing pattern with the kids at home, where it is helpful and where it might be hurtful. Reshape your focus in a way that is developmentally appropriate to their age, from helping them to helping them to help themselves. Practice the "sandwich spectrum" with them in various situations and create a new rhythm with it.

So much of a family's time in treatment includes the process of giving and receiving feedback and you can invite the kids at home into this process as well. Primarily, especially with younger kids, we encourage strengths-based feedback, which is found through the process of a "what's going well" meeting that we encouraged the use of at the end of Part 1. As not all feedback is positive and if you open the door to share some tougher stuff with each other, with an eye on modeling, we encourage you to receive feedback in the ideal way that you would hope your child does. You do not have to agree with it all or even respond to it. You can simply say, "tell me more, I can take it." And then, "Thanks. I'll think about all of that."

Now, this is a tool, not a rule, and is not meant for you to use if your child is being rude or verbally aggressive. If they are being aggressive *and* sharing feedback, after redirecting the moment and after some time has passed, you can have a brief repair in which you go to your child and say, "I was thinking about what you said and, while you could have said it differently, there is some truth to it and I am going to work on it."

Supporting siblings at home includes assessing how decisions are made. Over generations, we have seen the guiding focus for a family system shift from being fully parent-centered, where the day and week is prioritized around the parents' lives, to being more child-centered, where we aim to make happen whatever we need to for our children. The pendulum has perhaps swung a bit too far in a child-centered way, as we witness more and more entitled children and families that are run ragged by bending over backward to give them the lives they want. The family-focused approach allows for the whole family's needs to be prioritized with decision-making strategies that empower both parents and children.

During this time, with possibly the "easier" kids at home, invest in reviewing what your family's rhythm has been driven by, and envision what a family-centered approach might look like and what the cost is to you and your children if you stay more child or parent focused. The intention of the paradigm is meant also to help you shape the home in a way that can be more restorative for all and encourages parents to ask themselves, *who am I doing this for? Who does it benefit and to what end?*

A family-focused approach would encourage you to consider your own emotional currency, what you have to give without exhaustion and where you can encourage others to play an age-appropriate role; in this way you contribute to the growth of all of your children by helping them to help themselves.

Exercise

Try a "What's Going Well Meeting" this week. Within the next 48 hours, plan to sit down with your family and have everyone share one strength they have used in the past week to help the moments of their life go well. This can be a five-minute meeting or, if the conversation is going well, feel free to stretch it out. You can also invite everyone to share a strength they have seen in someone else. If it is just you or you and a co-parent, you can still make it happen.

Here are some sample strengths that you can use in your meeting.

Showing Kindness	Team Player	Loving
Being Loving	Great Communication	Flexible
Being Ambitious	Observed Leadership Opportunities	Humorous
Authentic	Writing Skills	Confident
Caring	Follows Directions Well	Grateful
Creative	Analytical	Accountable
Dedicated	Helping with Technology Skills	Respectful

Chapter 10

The Next Steps

By now, you and your child have been through a substantial part of the treatment journey and you are in the position of considering the next best steps to support their ongoing growth and stability. If your child is in a therapeutic boarding school or in residential treatment, you have done a deep dive into understanding the facets of your home, your parenting, and yourself that are important to you to shift or maintain. You have most likely been to the program for visits and possibly have even had a home visit if your child is in a residential treatment program. You have gathered information about how you interact with each other, what the emotions are beneath your "triggered" moments, what new skills you **enacted**, and which areas need more **mastery**.

Throughout this process, you have written and received many letters – for some of you less than you would prefer and for others more than you expected. You have been on the roller coaster of emotion driven by those exchanges where you have flopped from hopeless to hopeful. You have learned some of what has been beneath the surface for your child, and you have looked in the mirror to examine the role that you have played, ideally without taking on all the blame.

As a parent, you have worked on commitment to your family and learned to be honest about your strengths, struggles, needs, and hopes. You are considering recommendations and possibly starting to compare the support system you have at home for your child with longer term supportive treatment such as a therapeutic boarding school or a residential treatment center and you are about to start considering the risks and benefits of the options you have.

All parents involved are likely each concerned about what is next for your child and family, about the uncertainty of what the best decision is, how supportive it will be, and about how much it will cost. You are not alone. The decision about where a child goes after treatment can feel impossible at times. There are no certainties about how well your child or family will do in any situation, but you can take an honest look at the risks as well as the potential benefits of options available to you.

If, for example, your child has expressed the desire to be sober and has illustrated new tools relatively consistently, the risk of coming home might be lower. If they have continued to engage in self-harm throughout the program, then the risks are higher. If your child has substance abuse issues and you have parents in the home who are actively using and who are unwilling to have a dry home, then the risks are higher. We focus on this transition time so that you can reach clarity with your decision and help you feel prepared for whenever it is to come in the next few months.

Our expertise in this area will give you knowledge and hopefully challenge you to really dig deep into your parenting and your role, as you consider all options available to you and your child after wilderness therapy or an extended residential experience.

It's important to remember that parent and transition coaches like us will give you the confidence to bring your child home. Additionally, transition programs, like ours, are clearly in the business of bringing kids home. Personally, we are also in the business of making sure kids will have their needs served and will be successful if brought home. It's imperative that we challenge you to make a decision that will serve your child the best and that *you* allow our insights and guidance in this section to challenge you to make the best decision for you, your child, and your family. Just because there are a jillion reasons and numerous types of transition programs with countless ways to bring your child home, it doesn't always mean your child is going to be served best at home.

To help parents find their way as they decide where their child will transition to, we ask parents to thoughtfully look at the risks of their options and engage in a true cost-benefit analysis. To effectively do this, it is of utmost importance that you prioritize listening to and understanding the clinical assessments and recommendations that are provided to you while your child is in treatment. These clinical assessments and recommendations give you valuable information to truly assess the risk of your choices, and you can certainly choose to use them to inform your decision or not; just know those recommendations don't change, regardless of where your child transitions. Assessing risk through this lens is imperative, as it's the objective lens, there is no emotion in a clinical assessment.

Additionally, those assessments and recommendations will ground you in your considerations of all risks: risks of home, risk of public school, risk of a therapeutic boarding school, risk of her not being with the family, risk of her living with the family again. Assessing the risk from a practical, non-emotional perspective is crucial as you will find something out there that will confirm any emotional narrative you have in regards to what carries risk.

"We just got off another call with Tanya and she asked, yet again, when she can come home. We told her again that it is up to her, but we know, and so does she, that it is our decision, which we will make with the recommendation of her treatment team. But how *do* we know when she is ready?"

Our response to parents in this very common situation is to dig deep to find their answers: How do you know when *you* are ready—what does ready mean, who defines it, what do *you* need to be ready for?

The short answer to that last question is that you need to be ready to accept that your child has thankfully *not* had a lobotomy. She will come home herself, with some of the same thinking, behaviors, and temperament that you witnessed previously along with enhanced maturity, a new skill set, and increased awareness. Be ready to accept that all those new tools will be more challenging to practice with perseverance than she knows. She will not come home and be a high-functioning 30-year-old.

The short answer to the first question, "how you will know when *you* are ready?" is: when you have witnessed patterns of your own self-regulation and new responses to challenges, when you have increased awareness of what goes on beneath the surface for your child and for yourself. You will know, when your co-parenting team, if you have one, is measurably stronger in the support you are for each other and in **enacting** a middle ground approach to parenting, finding the sweet spot in between each of your perspectives.

Our belief that comes from years of experience in supporting parents in transition is that parents will and do shoulder the majority of the transition work and success. Ultimately this puts you, yes you, as the agents of change in your family system, in the position to be very clear about what you have learned, what is important for you to practice with perseverance, and what habits you can't fall back into.

A quick note on imperatives, as we are about to use some: we coach parents against using imperatives like, "you should" or "you need to" in their interactions with their children. Parents tend to use imperatives out of desperation, specifically when they are desperate to be heard or desperate to effect change. Unfortunately, the reality is that imperatives put the person on the receiving end in defense mode and impedes effective communication. As you read on, we ask that you hear our imperatives not from a defensive place, but with openness to hear them for what they are: essential and urgent.

If you are considering home as an option for you and your child, you need to be ready to commit, fully, with two feet in, to be resilient, to **master** the knowledge you have gained, and to **enact** new skills.

You need to be ready to set reasonable expectations and to steward a "let's keep trying" attitude, rather than expressing hopelessness when an incident occurs that reminds you of the past.

You need to be ready to distinguish between an incident and a pattern, to respond appropriately, and to do your best to not fall back into the same old patterns.

You need to be ready to be in the present, with a mind on the past, to help you predict pitfalls without allowing the fear of the past to resurface and to take over.

You need to be ready to make sacrifices, to take time to assess for yourselves what you are doing well and what areas need some added attention.

You need to be ready for the added stress that comes naturally with having a person who has been out of your system for some time, to have a physical presence in the home again.

You need to be ready for the intermittent anger and guilt trip your child will express about your willingness to have him out of your home.

You need to be able to maintain a weekly rhythm that also includes time for you to recover and refuel in healthy ways.

As you head into this next section, know that the focus is on transitioning a child home. If you are not at this point in your journey, then set this down and come back to it a month or two before he returns home. For those of you preparing to reunite at home, we encourage you to continue reading and allow the H.O.M.E. continuum to help with your own personal growth and to be your guide when you get to witness the new you, and identify the moments when the old you seeps in. When faced with a challenging moment, ask yourself if there is a skill you need to **hone**, a piece that you need to **own**, something that needs more practice for **mastery**, or something you have **mastered** that you need to remember to **enact**.

Remember. Reflect. Revisit.

- Accept the invitation to revisit your values.
- Shut up and love.
- Remember, you are a superhero.
- Find your people – they say it takes a village, but no one ever tells you where that is and when you can drop your kids off... you're still left with creating your own.
- When communicating, be the adult you hope your child grows to become.
- Put new tools into action with siblings at home.

Part 3

Master and Enact:
The Transition Home

Part 3

Master & Enact:
The Transition Home

This is the section for **mastering** your knowledge — identifying what you have learned and **mastering** your working knowledge of it so that you can then put it into action with confidence.

Reclaim the Parenting Baton

When you have a child in treatment, you have partially given away the baton of parenting, entrusting the program with the parenting of your child. You have done some parenting from afar, but they have held the baton more fully. Now, it is time to take it back, first by making a decision with the choices in front of you, then putting all you have learned into action. As you reclaim the baton, anchor back to your wise-minded parenting gut.

Through the sacred pause, you learned more about the voice of your parenting gut, when it is leaning more emotionally, when it is leaning toward the practical side and when it is in balance and thus coming from a wise-minded place. Knowing that the voice of your parenting gut is wise-minded and that it is not speaking from a place of your own trauma is key to reclaiming the baton. You can now know when you are acting as a loving parent and when you are rescuing your child to their detriment. You now know when you are **enacting** healthy communication and when you need to step back to **hone** the skill. You now know how to hold your child's upset with compassion while holding true to a healthy boundary.

With your decision to bring your adolescent or young adult home, you are ready to see and validate the moments of strength, in yourselves and in each other. You are ready to give your child a chance, within boundaries, to show you their growth. And you are ready for their growth to come in bits and pieces over time, not expecting it to always show up or not always show up in the moment. You have committed to re-define your role as a parent and allow for more balance, knowing when you need to parent and when you can coll-aborate, knowing where to honor your child's capabilities while encouraging more autonomy and independence. You now have the skills to be a patient cheerleader, a warrior, a role model, and to be gentle with yourselves as you all stumble your way forward. This is your moment of truth, and you are capable.

Alongside all your capabilities, there will be challenges and reminders that you have more to work on. During those moments of unnerving clarity, your antidote will be, to have a "let's keep trying" attitude. Simply, a willingness to act in a situation, to assess how it went, gather information, and to keep trying. We do this daily in other situations, whether in our professions, and with day-to-day tasks, though it can be tougher to **enact** with our struggling kids. We show up to a task as ready as we can be to take it on; things come our way and we manage them as we can and sometimes, we screw up.

When we do, we gather information, assess what went wrong and then get up with the willingness to try again. If you can approach things similarly at home and if you **master** a "let's keep trying" attitude, you **enact** a new tone that will not go unnoticed. And, as is the case with almost everything we teach, these are "tools, not rules" and everything needs moderation. Don't let your desire to have a "let's keep trying" attitude keep you from healthy boundaries or allow you to be taken advantage of. Be aware, use it in a wise-minded way.

Our hope is the guidance, suggestions, and exercises in Part 2, and the reminder of the importance of the sacred pause, has helped you to feel prepared as you **enact** your new skills in your child's transition home. Remember, you can always go back through those lessons in the times when you are compelled to find your inner warrior.

Chapter 11

Before Your Child Comes Home

To solidify your foundation for your next steps forward, this chapter focuses on concepts that can springboard you forward with more confidence.

Empower Yourself: Master Clarity Through Discernment

There are several questions to which the answers are important to know before your child leaves treatment. We have found that parents who can answer these questions with some detail show up better prepared to support their child in returning home. It is key that you are accountable for having a true understanding of these answers.

- What has your child learned through this process that is important to them?
- How do they see those things affecting their lives moving forward?

- Where is their level of **ownership** and accountability around past decisions and choices that led them to this current place of treatment?
- Where is their willingness to allow for your parenting, even when they disagree or dislike it?

When asked what we think anyone *should* gain from this process, while it is impossible to answer for so many unique situations, one statement we have identified as a general goal is for a young person to know when they truly need help, to know who the healthy people are to go to for help, to have the courage to ask for it, and finally, that they develop the willingness to incorporate the support they receive.

- Where do you think your child is with those abilities?
- Where do you think their true willingness is to allow for support?
- What will you need to incorporate in your home plan to support their abilities to do these things?

Another big question to chew on is: what exactly do you do with all of the information you learned about yourselves and that you received about your child?

Along with the observations from your child's treatment team, the breadth of information gleaned through the journey often includes psychoeducational testing, which offers parents and health and educational providers a window into the inner workings of your child. As transition specialists, we use that information to better understand how a child's brain interacts with the world around them and this informs parent coaching strategies that fit how a child processes information.

The testing report will also offer recommendations for tools and services to put into place to help your child continue on a healthy track. Parents can then find out what is possible to follow through with, based on the services in your area. We have already said this but cannot say it enough: this testing, along with information from your child's treatment team, can help you to identify the obstacles and the risks that you are facing and the level of support that those risks will necessitate.

To prevent the overwhelm that can come from this journey, we encourage you to make a list of what you have learned about your child's strengths and struggles as well as your own. We further encourage you to start working with your child's therapist and with your child to determine the top three to five recommendations important to follow through with, in order to prioritize the services that are most necessary to seek and make sure that you understand why.

For example, if a smaller classroom is recommended, what is it about their learning style that can benefit from this? If group therapy is recommended, what are the skills important to learn through group therapy? If some of the services are not available to you, like a smaller classroom, you can better understand the need it is meant to meet and determine if there are other options for meeting the needs.

Identifying the obstacles you will have to face when those recommended services at home are not available is crucial as you and the community in which you live will not be able to meet every therapeutic recommendation given. Knowing what you are going to do to prepare for those obstacles is of greater importance. You can make a chart, working with the treatment team, to extrapolate some of this with clarity and perhaps it will be effective to share it with your child. If you move forward with this, make sure to make a list of their strengths and why they matter as well.

As an example:

Child's needs/ recommendation from testing	Why it matters	Obstacles we face if services are not available
Small classroom	*Attentional struggles and social anxiety that make accessing his intelligence a challenge*	*Need to tie in added 1-1 support, executive functioning coach*
Social skills training	*Missing cues and hyper focusing on self gets in the way of relationships which is negatively impacting self-esteem and contributes to depression*	*Our child's loneliness; our belief they are lonely when 1 or 2 friends might be enough for them; our child feeling bullied or bullying*

Child's Strengths	Why it matters
High visual-spatial capability	*Helps with seeing the big picture, understanding big concepts; great imagination and helps with spelling and geometry*
Integrity	*Does what is right even when no one is looking; earns trust easily*

 **Nugget of Knowledge:** When you feel overwhelmed by what you think you don't know, make a list of 10 pertinent things you do know. This helps soothe the panic and engages your brain in a way that incorporates a fuller picture of the truth and can lead to a decrease in stress.

Define Success

Parents tend to spend a significant amount of time defining what they see as their child's success and the reality is that you as a parent only have control over your own. Spending time defining what being successful looks like for you *and* your child will assist you in acknowledging where you have control, how effective your expectations are and if *you* are truly setting *yourself* up for success.

Success is complex because it's subjective, and the good news is, you get to define what success looks like for you and what your vision of success looks like for your child(ren). Having a different response, redirecting yourself sooner when you don't, using more intentional skill, and creating less damage in the relationship than in the past, as examples, are great ways to define success. Remember the statement, if you want to change your life, change the meaning that you place on things? And the bit about waiting to place meaning on things until time passes to allow more puzzle pieces to come together? As you start to define success, those can be helpful to incorporate.

Consider taking the first steps by envisioning your own success, as a person, as a parent, as a co-parent. Consider projecting to 90 days from this moment, what does it look like to you, what are you hoping for? As you project into the future, imagine being in your ideal relationship with your child, and with your family as a whole, while contemplating how hard it has been and how far you have come. You believe you have done all you can and that it has gone relatively well. You define it as a success. Now, ask yourself, what is it that I put into action to help it go as well as it did? What have I **honed**, **owned**, **mastered**, and **enacted** to help things go well?

Knowing where you are going can help you outline the steps to get there. There are many different ways to set goals as you aim for your success, SMART goals being one example that have been around for a long time and have been used in many different contexts. The process of setting a SMART goal guides you to define goals that are specific, measurable, achievable, relevant, and time-bound. The primary purpose is to make clear and measurable goals and to set yourself up for success with achieving them. While the goals toward which you and your family are working might seem abstract, it is important to identify the concrete aspects so that you can make them measurable, effectively assess your progress and identify the obstacles that might get in the way of your success.

As an example:

Specific goal	I will celebrate and validate more than I criticize myself and others
Measurable	I will focus on this for two weeks and make hash marks in a notepad each time I do it
Achievable	I will aim for two validating, celebratory comments a day
Relevant	I want to change the tone of my home with what I have control over
Time-bound	I will do this for two weeks and assess how I am doing and how it is helping

Knowing that you only have control over you, you simultaneously know that you want to influence how your children define their own success. To be able to effectively influence as a parent, your participation in conversations surrounding goals must include your willingness to listen. It will be helpful to listen to their definitions of success with curiosity rather than judgment. You do not have to be the wet blanket to challenge their lofty goals or express disappointment if the bar is not as high as you would prefer. Just listen.

Certainly, if her goals include being a drug dealer, you might not want to smile and say, "tell me more." You can say, "that's a bummer! I hope you make different choices because you have greater gifts to offer the world." And, if your child continues down that unhealthy path, it is important that parents have clear boundaries to define when you need to intervene more directly. Take the time to think about how you would define success for them.

- Are the goals you envision for your child feasible?
- Are they necessary as you look at the next three to six months?
- Are they truly beneficial and to what end?
- Are you focused on them getting into med school or are you focused on them making better decisions in the day to day?

Taking notes on this can help you to see where your expectations might be lofty, which will impact your interactions when your disappointment leaks out sideways.

While you might believe that you have defined success for your child with reasonable expectations, your responses in moments of disappointment might illustrate otherwise. You can prove that you have realistic expectations and highlight your own growth through changing the meaning you place on the disappointment-filled moments. Kim John Payne in "The Soul of Discipline", offers a paradigm shift for parents to support this process. He opens the book by reframing the paradigm of the disobedient child with the concept of them being disoriented. By seeing your child as someone who is disoriented and who needs a response from you to reorient on track, rather than seeing them as simply disobedient, you can choose your actions more wisely.

We cannot tell you how many times we have referenced this to exhausted, fearful, angry, hurt parents. Payne writes, "Just as a submarine navigator gets his or her bearings by sending out sonic pings that bounce off underwater objects and orient the ship to rocks or reefs, our children send out 'pings' in the form of challenging behavior." When children send out pings, parents are responsible for responding with the information that will help them to orient themselves back to safety. When you consider this paradigm, you have a better chance at **owning** and **enacting** a helpful action in response, rather than an unhealthy reaction.

To even further augment the chances of a healthy reaction, you can **enact** the three C's: being clear, concise, and consistent. This is a concept we taught as wilderness therapists and one in which effectiveness shines through when parenting. Your clarity sharpens by knowing what values you want to orient your child to and you **own** it with two feet in by offering a clear, concise, consistent response to the situation that has them heading for danger. You then **master** this paradigm shift, remembering the disoriented vs. disobedient idea and you **enact** new responses.

The concept of success can also be tied into the day-to-day as you learn ways to set yourself and your family up for success. This requires awareness and a process of assessing when things go wrong and when things go right. When something goes right, ask yourself what you did to help it go well or what about the situation itself was a set up for success. When something goes poorly from your estimation, could you have done something to better set everyone up for success? It might not solve everything, but it is good practice nonetheless. Investing and continuing in good practices such as these will strengthen your responses and handling of situations.

Realistic Expectations

It is critical for you to acknowledge that there are unrealistic expectations you might have and that you may need to spend time reassessing and consider loosening the reins a bit. Some are about you, some about your child, some about the support you will have moving forward. To be able to see where your expectations are realistic or not, you will need to truly understand the difference between expectations and boundaries which are often misconstrued as one in the same.

Owning Your Engagement: Sue's experience.

Sue, like many parents we work with, interchanged the words "boundary" and "expectation" and was getting caught up in how to successfully implement both when it came to being in conflict with her kids. As we broke down the engagements she was having, we focused on making a distinction between the two and she decided that she was no longer going to participate in conversations with her children, or with anyone for that matter, who were yelling and cussing at her during conflict.

She was then able to identify that her boundary was her unwillingness to participate in these conversations when this was happening. She did not have control over how her children engaged when there was conflict, but she recognized she could control her participation, which was to implement her boundary and allow the other person to make adjustments to her established boundary, her unwillingness to participate. She also was clear she could make this an expectation with her children, the expectation that they engage in respectful communication even when they are angry and upset with her.

What made her expectation realistic is that, while holding her boundary of not participating in the conversation when she was being yelled at and cussed at by her son, she later was able to follow the realistic expectation up with an action. The action was putting a consequence in place to help redirect his style of engagement for the next time they found themselves in conflict.

An easy way to distinguish the two is that a boundary is yours to establish for yourself that others must adjust to while an expectation is something you put on someone with the assumption that they will meet it. If we establish a boundary for how we communicate for example, even when others push against that boundary, our only response is to fortify within ourselves the boundary that is important to us while allowing those around us to find their way to accepting and adjusting to it.

To identify how realistic and doable your expectations are to implement, consider these two rules: if you are placing an expectation on your child, you will need to identify how you will measure and monitor them to see if they are meeting your expectation and you will need to be prepared to have a response that requires an action plan from you when they don't follow or meet your expectation. If you can't identify what this response will be then it may not be an expectation you should put into place.

Enacting New Communication Styles

We think there is great value in spending more time looking at the different communication styles and parenting styles and how they are connected. The three styles of communication often referenced are passive, assertive, and aggressive.

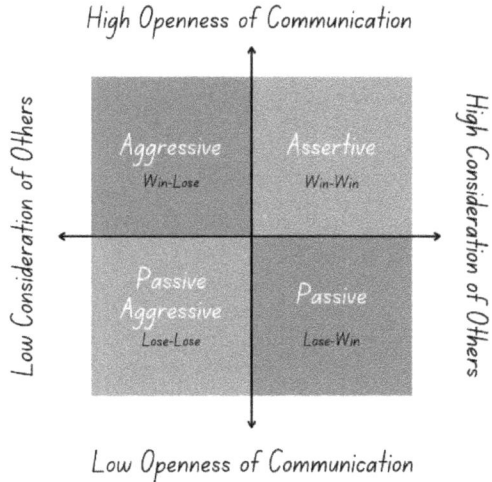

Communication Styles

Illustration based on the Four Communication Styles.

Similarly, the three styles of parenting are permissive, authoritative, and authoritarian. There is a connection between how we communicate and the style of parenting that we engage in. Even if we don't desire to be permissive or think we are not permissive in our parenting, if we are passive in our communication then permissiveness is often implied. The same goes for aggressive communication and the authoritarian parenting style.

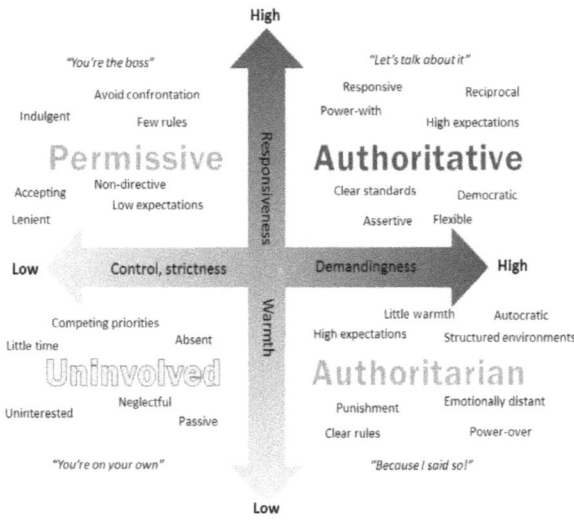

Parenting Styles

Illustration used with permission by Graeme Stuart.

When we engage in the constant "you" statements and one-way conversations that are filled with lectures, we are implying an authoritarian style of parenting that screams "the only way to do something is 'my way'." Assertive communication allows us the opportunity to find ourselves more consistently in the role of an authoritative parent; the parent who is clear about their boundaries as well as being clear about their ability to engage in an emotionally connected relationship with their children, while still holding those clear boundaries.

The three C's, being clear, concise, and consistent play an important role here as well and really is a staple in communication for all parents. For those over-communicators and those parents who spend a lot of time using a lot of words to make your child "feel better" about what you are about to say, this concept is for you. For those of you who tend to be passive in your communication and less assertive, this concept is for you. And for those of you who tend to lecture or to start your sentences off with "you should"' when talking to your child, this concept is for you.

Let's sidestep into "should" for a minute, as such a small word can represent such a heavy message. Something that is a "should" for you, might not be true for someone else and the act of "shoulding" on someone can disempower and can deliver the message that others cannot find their way on their own. We can "should" ourselves into shame and negative self-thought, thus making shaky our own foundation. When you hear yourself using a "should", ask yourself what the message is that you are trying to communicate, if it is a truly necessary and wise-minded message, and then find a way to reword it, whether you are talking to yourself or to someone else.

You can say, for example, "it might be good to consider..." Take the time to figure out what is important about the message you are conveying and find words that fit for you, leaving the "should" out of it. As parents, you often have a clear understanding of the decisions you would make for your children. You have the experience, the foresight, the more fully-developed brains. You also know that sitting your kids down and telling them what they should do rarely works. Now, this does not mean you lose the opportunity to influence, teach, and guide your children; the goal is to shape your message with new language that might have a better chance of being received.

When you use a concept like the 3 C's, you allow yourself the opportunity to live in a more authoritative way in your parenting, the ideal style of parenting. Being clear, concise, and consistent in your communication forces you to have clear intent behind your choice of words and the message you are attempting to communicate. Being concise offers you the opportunity for your message to be heard in a clear way, even when the message is undesirable to hear. Consider how short the attention span can be, especially for younger kids or when walls are up to protect from discomfort. And being consistent, offers you the opportunity to hit repeat to help you practice implementing your boundaries and commitments.

Know Your Position as a Parent

Knowing where you stand on an issue as a parent and a co-parenting team takes a considerable amount of self-reflection and engagement with one another to figure out what you believe, what you value, what you think. It should be intellectual conversations that allow you to identify your positions as a parent. In these conversations, you should come to an understanding as to how you will find shared attitudes and commitments in the different areas of parenting. It also requires you to consider all the areas where you need to have a position as a parent, such as education, drug and alcohol use and/or experimentation, dating, and electronic and social media use.

When these intentional exercises and conversations do not happen, parents tend to make emotional decisions in their parenting because there is not a clear, agreed upon stand-point to parent from. Without that clarity, we get desperate and scramble for control which ultimately leads to reacting rather than responding. When we react, we parent from a place of emotion and when we respond, we parent from the place that confirms the steadiness in our decisions.

Clarifying Parenting Positions: Jeff & Mindy's experience.

Jeff and Mindy found their position around curfews through intentional conversations about their own childhood experiences that gave them direction in where they could stand together on this topic as a co-parenting team. Setting a blanket curfew to one parent reminded them of when they literally sat in the park close to their childhood home, not always making the best decisions and often not really doing anything but staying out only because they didn't have to be home until a certain time every night.

They, as a co-parenting team, decided they didn't really believe in the blanket curfew time and identified that their position was one that allowed for flexibility, encouraging their kids to engage with them about the activity they were asking to do so they could determine what the curfew was for that particular night. Their position also allowed for them to parent in the moment when their child would become frustrated with not having a blanket curfew so they could remind him, "if you want a blanket curfew, you may have it, but it will be early, if you want to talk about your plans and give us more information, you will have a better chance of staying out later."

Finding your parenting position is similar to a basketball player who comes to a stop on the court, they have options from the place they decided to be in. They can dribble, they can pivot, they can shoot, they have options as they stand firm, making decisions from that place. If they are not clear about their position, then their next step will be to travel without direction. Wouldn't it be great if there was someone to blow a whistle on us every time we travel as a parent without a planned direction?

The Hat You Wear

One gift of being human is that we can show up in different ways based on the situation. Going to a football game, going to a musical or Thanksgiving dinner, being in your own space at home… you likely act differently in each situation and in some ways, play a different role, wear a different hat. There are many hats we wear in the day-to-day life of parenting. One is your parenting hat and the other is your mom or dad hat. Let's look at how and why we make the distinction.

Your parenting hat is like the hat you wear to work; it is your job. With your parenting hat on, you are able to deal with the issue in front of you by responding intellectually and you are able to implement tools like being clear, concise, and consistent in your messaging. The emotion is put aside when you wear this hat, which allows you to make decisions from an intellectual place, not an emotionally reactive place.

The key is to learn the skill, which is not always innate, of putting emotion aside for even a few minutes, to captain the ship toward what is best for the child or family. With your parenting hat on you parent the issue and then take space for yourself to return to the emotion and manage what you have going internally.

The mom or dad hat is the fun hat you get to wear, full of emotion and connection, even saying yes to things you might not normally. When you have this hat on you can be emotionally connected with your child, you get to have fun, you get to engage and practice your skills of attunement, and hopefully you get to laugh and play when you are wearing this hat.

It's not feasible to wear these hats simultaneously, as our emotions while wearing our mom or dad hat will interfere when wearing our parenting hat. It's similar to trying to wear two baseball hats at one time, we can pull it off for a few seconds, but it doesn't take long for one to fall off when we take a step.

To see the clear distinction of these roles for yourself, take the time and really identify what you want to look like while wearing your parenting hat, how you want to engage, what intentional position you are parenting from. Have a clear lens to how it differs from what you want to look like when you get to wear your mom or dad hat.

 **Nugget of Knowledge:** We need emotion to be a parent but when we parent with emotion, we trip ourselves up. This is a crucial statement parent coaches like us often share with and remind parents.

Acceptance & the Myth of Letting Go

For a child to thrive in the home environment after a treatment experience, especially for a child who has made significant efforts in his own self-awareness and account-ability, a parent has to accept that the responsibility is on the parent to change the environment, their responses, and how they engage in the relationship. A child demonstrating evidence that "a different kid is coming back", is reliant on his parents to know how to interact and respond to this new person coming home.

Abraham Maslow's theory on the hierarchy of needs ends with self-actualization, the ability to become the best version of oneself. Maslow stated, "This tendency might be phrased as the desire to become more and more of what one is, to become everything one is capable of becoming." The **mastery** of your own newfound skills will ensure you can support your child as he attempts to sustain his. One of the main characteristics of a self-actualizer is the practice of acceptance, one of the greatest areas a parent needs to define their success in.

There are many challenges in finding acceptance as a parent, one specifically being our attachment to outcomes. In the therapeutic world, parents are often advised to learn to "let go of the outcome." The reality is we are very attached to the outcomes of our children and "letting go" of those attachments is not easy. We are attached to the outcome that they will have friends, that that will make good choices, that they will be the athlete we predicted they could be, that they will perform a certain way in school and even attached to the outcome of how we hope they will "turn out" as adults.

The story we have witnessed time and again that illustrates this topic is when we hear about parents completing their children's schoolwork.

"Charlie got to a point where he was so behind, and I imagined that it was hard for him to see the light at the end of the tunnel. He seemed to be giving up and just hung out with his friends and played on the PS4. We thought that when he was told by his coach he may not be able to play on the baseball team, which was something he always loved, that it would motivate him but it didn't. I did not want him to lose that healthy outlet and I wanted him to be able to get through sophomore year and have a better shot at graduating with his peers on time and so I started to complete his work for him. I figured that, if I could get him caught up and help him stay on the baseball team that he would be able to start fresh next year and have a better chance at staying on top of things."

This story highlights how parents often over function for their children, so tied to the outcomes, that they try to put the band aid on to help the immediate pain, while not supporting a healthy long term solution. And, of course, when his junior year started, Charlie was soon in the same position as he had been the year before, having not managed the underlying challenges nor learning from the previous year's struggles.

 **Nugget of Knowledge:** The reality is that when one person over functions in a relationship, the other person is left to under function.

The work for parents is to recognize your own attachments to these outcomes, accept that you do have them and discern what part of your child achieving that outcome is in your control. This is the "how" part of the therapeutic encouragement to "let go" of the outcome – you don't necessarily let go of the attachment to the outcome, but rather get super clear about how much control you as a parent actually have over that outcome to which you are so attached. Parents who say they can "let go" of an attachment to an outcome can only do so if they truly understand what part of the outcome they can control.

Additionally, parents need to go through the process of feeling the discomfort and accepting the emotions that come with the realization that those outcomes we are attached to may not be achieved. When this latter step doesn't occur, it will impede a parent's ability to be that best, self-actualized version of themselves. It can keep parents enmeshed, not seeing where they as a parent end and their child begins and it will keep a parent in the role of over functioning in the relationship, all to "ensure" the outcome they are attached to for their child is met.

Conditional Creatures

The great war of parent and adolescent relationships is the clash of unconditional parents and conditional kids. We like to call kids in this developmental stage, "conditional creatures" because, developmentally, they have grown into something parents often don't recognize. The moment your baby arrived, you most likely became selfless and unconditional as a parent. The conditional clash that later occurs happens when we want this unconditional love reciprocated by our children. You remember, the type they gave when they were little, expressing unconditional love, wanting to be around us, wanting us to participate in their daily activities, and so on. But now, the conditional creatures they become, starting in middle childhood, only want us around or show their love when they want something.

In our work supporting parents with struggling teens and older adolescents, otherwise known as emerging young adults, we spend time making the distinction between what are clinically significant behaviors and what are challenging, but age-appropriate behaviors. One very age-appropriate behavior is that our adolescents are egocentric, conditional in relationships, and often take more than they give. This is hard to swallow, and the resistance parents often have during this phase has indeed created one of the biggest obstacles in parenting.

This resistance naturally happens as most adults consciously choose only to engage in relationships that are reciprocated. As adults, we typically don't keep friends in our circle that only talk to us when we take them out to dinner or only call us back when they want something from us. We are not accustomed to being in conditional relationships and thus are taken off guard when our daily interactions with the ones we love do not feel mutual.

Culturally, it makes sense that they have morphed into a more conditional mindset. Grades, trophies, allowance, and social media are all the conditional systems that make up their world.

With their focus becoming internalized, at this age, they start to figure out their boundaries and values. Taking into consideration their limited perspective, the conditions they place on relationships make sense. The more that we, as parents, understand and accept that this is part of the normal child-rearing picture, the less surprised, upset, and reactive you will be when it happens. More importantly, the less personally we take this phase, the better chance we have of staying attached and attuned to them when it gets difficult.

Nugget of Knowledge: They are conditional in all of their relationships during this developmental stage; you are just impacted the most because you remain unconditional in your love.

Here are some basic do's and don'ts when navigating your relationship with your child during this often long developmental stage. Frequently, to maintain the feeling of closeness with our conditional creatures, parents flex and bend and do backflips in their over-giving, hoping that the child will, in turn, shift their conditional approaches. Keep your boundaries; don't do backflips. Takers will always take, so you as the giver need to follow your own boundaries within the giving. The concept you have already been introduced to and we teach parents over and over is to always anchor to your values with your wise mind.

Know what you *are* and *are not* willing to give in the relationship. Parents, in wise-minded ways, think through the emotional and the rational, the pros and cons, of situations whenever possible *before* responding to a child's request or demand. Take the time you need to get into the wise mind before addressing a situation so that you are less reactive to the conditions you are on the receiving end of.

Role model and teach reciprocity and relational con-sequences. A parent recently wrote an email to his parent coach on our team:

They always say that the best time you have to talk to your kids is in the car and so I always try to be the parent giving rides to Sophie and her friends. She has been in the habit lately of being abusive; yes, there is the typical teen sarcasm, but it has also crossed a line into attacking comments such as, 'too bad you lost your hair 10 years ago, dad, you might have been able to find a girlfriend.' And she says this with her friends in the car! I don't want to lose out on time spent together, but how much of this do I need to take?

His coach, in an effort to illustrate that responding with healthy boundaries is good modeling, suggested that the next time he is asked to give them a ride, he say, "You know, I was pretty hurt by how you treated me last time, and so this time the answer is no, but we can give it another try tomorrow." This models healthy reciprocal relationships, suggests cause and effect, and shows that recovery *is* possible, and you are willing to try again.

Remember the sandwich spectrum? This is another and lighter way to teach reciprocity. If they always ask you to make them a snack, make them a snack sometimes, but other times you can shift into offering to do it together and even ask them to make a snack for you!

Part of your role through all of this is to role model the adult you hope they grow to become. You do not want your child to think that it is healthy to treat people poorly and still get what they want. Of course, some acceptance of the adolescent-parent conditional reality is to be expected. But it is vital that you identify a line that you are not willing to let them cross and get away with it. While you might just get an eye roll now, it is important to remember that this is the long game; the efforts you put in now help to set the stage for tools they can better access once they are more developed and mature. This is no different than telling your kids over and over that you love them in times when they are not willing to hear it so that they can anchor back to that when they are older.

At this point, we have shared concepts that we spend many months **honing** and **mastering** with parents during the transition home. It is a lot. Chunk it down to what matters most for you right now. Take the opportunity to truly consider how the guidance we give applies to you and what knowledge you do have to incorporate in the changes you are making for yourself and your family. Highlight the eye openers that provide you reassurance, confidence and even relief. Come back to this section as you need to, reminding yourself that you are human and not meant to be robotic in your therapeutic knowledge and execution, you are just meant to absorb it, consider it, and use what is helpful.

Remember. Reflect. Revisit.

- Tap back into your wise-minded parenting gut and reclaim the parenting baton with confidence.
- Before your child comes home, get clear on what you know and don't, about your child in treatment, yourselves, your family.
- Examine how you define success – yours and your child's.
- Anchor to your values; **hone, own, master,** and **enact** from a clear parenting position.

Chapter 12

Predict & Prepare to Enact Your Home Plan

This chapter focuses on predicting common pitfalls and identifying tools to manage them with grace.

He is coming home. Now what? Depending on your style, you may even add a few expletives to that statement. No matter how long your child has been in treatment, eight weeks, 16 weeks, eight months, there is much to prepare for. From our perspective, it's where the rubber meets the road for you as a parent, maybe even more so than for your child. The amount of preparation you commit to will be reflected through your actions and ability to put theory into realistic practice.

At this point, you need to predict and prepare for situations coming down the road as well as establish agreements for living together. It's important for you to know what you can predict and prepare for, to remember that you have a new skill set and to make sure you know that your family has put too much time, energy, emotion, and money toward this process to let things break down with the return of hold habits.

It is not wise to depend on your child's changes to change the tone of the whole home. Claim your role, **own** it.

Look back through all of your notes that you have taken during their treatment process and identify the themes that repeat. Look at acronyms you have gone back to time and again and find the aspects that have staying power because they fit for you. Write those bullet points down on a sticky note, fill 10 sticky notes if you can, and put them all over your room. Do what you need to in order to keep all that you have learned in mind. You most likely will be upset when your child loses sight of what they have learned, but all you can do is resist the temptation of falling out of the habits yourself.

If you identify predictable challenges ahead of time, you have even more resources to collaborate and solve problems as they arise. You also are able to make a plan that fits your values to manage the predictable, which frees up some emotional currency when these situations surface.

The transition, and preparation for it, is the time to identify the top skill areas that you want to **master** to assess them consistently after your child is home to make sure the skills are still pertinent. After so much time talking about these skills, you are now faced with the opportunity to **enact** them in real time and see how well you execute. To support you with **enacting** those new skills, we will help you to predict some common situations and help you to prepare for them with some of our tools and tips.

 **Nugget of Knowledge:** Even if you think that you have already talked through your child's frustration about your decision to intervene and have him out of your home, it will resurface and it is normal. It will be triggered in various ways during the first several months following a transition. Your job is to listen and to say, "we really hope that you feel differently one

day and that you can see it from our perspective, but we understand that you can't right now."

Predicting Common Traps

"There's a Hole in my Sidewalk: The Romance of Self-Discovery" by Portia Nelson is a great poem often used in treatment to address the importance of self-awareness. It challenges our autopilot approach to life that keeps us repeating actions that don't serve us and it encourages transformation. Reading it through our parenting eyes, it reminds us of the all-too-common traps parents fall into, which continue to ignite conflict and keep parents upending the work they are doing as they walk the path of change. Luckily, at least a few of those traps that might be ahead of you are predictable, which means that you can prepare for them.

The "You Don't Trust Me" Trap

The "you don't trust me" trap occurs when you as the parent want to draw a boundary to help facilitate a healthy transition and your child battles back with the statement, "you don't trust me", which could be expanded to, "what was the point of being in treatment for so long if you won't let me do anything?" Trust is a hot topic, especially with kids who have gone through a treatment experience and have been rather successful.

This place they find themselves in is sometimes referred to as the "wilderness/treatment high" and is filled with excitement about authentic changes, genuine hopes, and plans for their new life, all which lead them to a belief of automatic trust from their parents. They see trust as black and white, "you either trust me or not" and the reality is that trust has many facets, many interpretations, and many components when one is determining the level of a trust in a relationship or just in someone's decision making.

Adolescents, no matter how intelligent they are, tend to be more concrete thinkers and their thinking tends to be focused on the present. There is a developmental time period that lasts much longer than most parents are comfortable with, which is called the invincibility fable. Simply, when kids live life as if nothing bad will happen to them. This fable they live in increases the intensity of their stance on why you should have blanket trust in them.

The "you don't trust me" trap will usually start before your child leaves treatment during conversations about how the future will look.

"You are going to drug test me? I can't believe after all I have done here that you don't trust me."

"Clearly you don't trust me if I have to follow all of these rules, why should I bother even coming home?" is another common favorite. And with that, the trap has been set by your child who has made authentic changes, who desperately wants to come home and is still going to see if these emotional baits will still trap you into changing your mind about a rule you want to put into place.

Our experience has been that the majority of parents really struggle with the topic of trust with their children and usually it's because of their own discomfort in having to admit that they actually don't trust them. This discomfort is amplified when a child has worked so hard in treatment and the memories of their past decisions are appropriately fading as they are replaced with the new experiences of success in treatment.

Parents tend to stumble their way through this, back on their heels, back on eggshells, responding with, "No, no, it's not that I don't trust you, you *have* earned trust." We ask parents to really think about whether or not they *do* have blanket trust in their children and, if not, why is it so hard to be honest about it? The gray nature of trust allows a parent to say, "well, you have earned some trust and in this specific situation, I need more experience with you to trust that you will make the best decisions and for me to feel assured that it is worth the risk right now." By being honest that they have earned some trust but that they still have some work to do at home, you help them orient to a wise-minded reality of the situation.

Reliability and integrity are components of trust that are built over time and your child needs time with you as they transition from the treatment environment back into this "new" home environment. Often an extensive period of time and clear expectations are needed to show how reliable they are, to do what they say they are going to do. And it's more than okay for you as a parent to ask for that, for time to see that reliability, time to see how your child incorporates all that she has learned in her current environment into her new one. Remember, adolescence is a time for instant gratification and concrete thinking, you as an adult are not in that place which allows you to use time to ensure the trust they are asking for is worth the risk.

It can be helpful to identify the areas where you do have trust in your child and areas you don't that need more time to assess their reliability. It can also be helpful to find your way by sitting in the discomfort – that you actually don't trust your adolescent – more comfortably.

The "Blind to What's Beneath" Trap

Let's invite the old "tip of the iceberg" adage here and keep in mind that what you see above the surface is only a snippet of what lies beneath. When things are moving quickly and the behavior is what you see above the surface, you can quickly forget all that you learned is beneath the surface for your child and respond to the behavior as though it is the whole of what is happening. As parents working to shape the tone of the home in new ways, your job with this trap is to slow down, use curiosity and, before you take a stand in a situation, consider what might be beneath the surface.

Quite often, adolescents can be verbally compliant while being behaviorally oppositional and it can create confusion and frustration to those in relationship with them. Your child's behavior that has that oppositional flare, especially after they have agreed to something, can ignite a parent's reactive side, negatively affecting access to skills like curiosity and wise mindedness.

Look Beneath the Surface: Sam & Tamyra's experience.

Sam and Tamyra had a young adult at home. They had a history of high anxiety, had few friends, and at times had an oppositional attitude. Their parents agreed to give them a car to help them build independence and part of the agreement was that the child needed to wash it twice a month. Sam and Tamyra told them they could pay to bring it to the car wash, or they could save their money and wash it at home. They were not following through, and their parents were fuming about what they viewed as their child's entitlement and lack of care for the things they gave them.

"Have they ever washed a car?" we asked. "Was it a chore they did as a kid, or have they ever been driving when you went through the car wash?" As we gathered more infor-mation, we learned that in fact they had very few chores as a child and neither parent could think of a time when their child washed a car, though they could come up with moments when they had been a passenger when they went through the drive through car wash.

We spoke about their child's anxiety in general and the complexities of being a young driver; these were aspects Sam and Tamyra took for granted as they saw it as such a simple task. We intentionally broke down the details of this expectation to better understand the behind-the-scenes work a brain does, which are simply automatic for experienced adults:

- driving up close enough but not too close to the machine;
- the possibility of having to go inside to get a code first;
- choosing the right wash with the three to five options outlined;
- managing a salesperson at the car wash encouraging a more expensive wash;
- driving the car the right way to get the tire onto the conveyor belt, knowing when to get the car in neutral and when to get it back in drive on the tail end.

All of this plays out with a backdrop of anxiety, which can often feel debilitating to those experiencing it and can be a major obstacle to accessing the skills that one does have.

The major misunderstanding was the belief that it was their young adult's oppositionality and not their anxiety that was the obstacle to follow through. This situation allowed the opportunity to apply a version of the well-known approach "Connect and Redirect" from the book "No Drama Discipline." Connect first, with curiosity, then redirect with solutions or consequences if needed, once a relational connection has been made.

The connect then redirect approach is important for many situations. It allows a dysregulated brain, which in this case was the opposition their parents saw being activated by their child's severe anxiety, to quiet down to access all of its functions, when their parents approached them in a connective way through curiosity. This led to them being able to soothe their thoughts, problem solve, and use logic when communicating what they needed, which was for their mom to go with them a couple of times to help them feel more confident and competent to follow through with the expectation, which they did with relative ease after the support.

The "Taking the Bait" Trap

Another predictable situation and classic trap for which you may want to plan and prepare for are interactions where you might "take the bait" as a parent. Taking the bait refers to communication where you are perhaps trying to hold your child accountable and they dangle a baited hook in an attempt to redirect the conversation, often aimed at avoiding accountability. This might sound like:

Parent: "You were 15 minutes late for curfew, so you are not going out tomorrow night."

Child: "Mom, I was only 11 minutes late; you always exaggerate so you can just punish me more."

Parent: "That is not true, I don't always exaggerate to punish you, I simply want to hold you to our agreements."

Child: "You do. You *always* — remember when I got a C and you..."

Parent: "No, when you got that C, I..."

At this point, the conversation focus is effectively shifted to whether or not mom exaggerates, and it is no longer about the child being late for curfew. Success, the bait has been taken and most likely the accountability avoided. When you find yourself in this position, which you will, use the skills you have been practicing, specifically around buying time and captaining your ship through response vs. reaction.

What to do instead? Be a zen master who does not need to defend themselves when the baited hook is dangled. "You're right, you were home 11 minutes late, not 15 and maybe tomorrow we can make a plan together to get you home on time in the future." When you agree with a point that is low risk, such as whether your child is 11 or 15 minutes late, you can move back to your focus without a distracting power struggle.

Also, consider holding off on implementing consequences immediately, it's okay to wait until the next day – If you welcome your child home, ask if they had fun and say, "it looks like you are a bit late, but we can talk about it tomorrow." You then buy yourself and your child time, decrease the chances of an emotionally reactive response and give everyone a chance of showing up better for the harder conversation after a good night's sleep.

Taking the bait can happen over thousands of situations and it is identifiable during most power struggles where you can hear yourself in a tit for tat or back and forth arguing a point.

It shares similarity to our guidance of not **owning** accusations. Adolescents throw accusations around for the same reason, often to avoid responsibility or accountability. It can surface in comparisons that they make between how you treat them or what you expect from them in comparison to their sibling(s). It surfaces by throwing accusations such as "you said you were going to change and you didn't do any work while I was away," attempting to cripple you emotionally in hopes it may steer you away from focusing on the issue at hand.

The most successful way to not take this type of bait is to be clear with yourself that you don't have to "**own** the accusation" and just because it was said, does not make it true. That simple, yet difficult redirection of your own thoughts being fueled by deep emotion in that moment, when the bait has been thrown, will allow you to apply many of the tools you have to effectively address the situation at hand.

Adolescents feel disempowered often, and much of that is due to how society has viewed and treated them. They are often underestimated while craving a sense of purpose and treated with implied incapability while being pressured to be responsible. As a result, they try to feel power in unhealthy ways, as feeling power in healthy ways can be a bit more challenging and can require more work. So, when they can derail a conversation and get you to take the bait, it can feel powerful.

Your job is to notice when you are contributing by staying stuck in an unnecessary back and forth. If you think it is a necessary back and forth, it is important that, afterward, you take the time to truly understand what was so necessary about it and why it needed to happen in the time frame you thought it did. There are times when the power struggle is necessary for a period of time, but it usually drags on for longer than is useful and parents are just as guilty as kids are with trying to get the last word in. **Own** your part so you can **enact** new responses to notice the bait and leave it dangling.

The "Reacting to Tone" Trap

"It's not what you say, it's how you say it." Parents are universally annoyed by the tone with which kids react. It is imperative to acknowledge that you as a parent, as the adult, get to decide what you participate in and how. Just as you get to decide whether to stick around and participate in a conversation filled with tone, you get to decide how you will participate.

How a parent participates is based on the internalization process of this work you are investing in as well as your willingness and ability to catch yourself and redirect when you realize you may have chosen an approach to participation that is not serving you or your child. **Mastering** new responses to this can help you shape the tone of your home in ways that leave you feeling more fueled than drained.

It is important to identify if a child is being overly aggressive with name calling, loudness, or if they are communicating with an attitude to either feel in power, push you away, or at times, when they don't even know they are. If the former is the case, then it is important for parents to draw a clearer line while still offering the child an opportunity to course correct.

This might sound like, "There is something important you are trying to share with me, and I will keep listening and might even agree with some of what you are saying, if you can stop cursing and name calling." If it continues, draw your line, perhaps even with a hand up in a "stop" motion and say something like, "I can't participate in this conversation when you are being hurtful, I am walking away, and we can find time to try again later."

If your child is communicating with a tone that you would simply not prefer, then we encourage a couple of directions. The first is to respond to content, not tone. There are times when it makes sense to just let it go so you are not trying to teach them about their tone every time you interact. Try not to take it personally and remember that your child is a developing little human who is in the process of forming and the tone they use with you may not be something that they carry into interactions with others or into adulthood. You do not need to worry about their ability to get a job in the future based on their response to, "what homework do you have tonight?" So, consider responding to content as though you were tone deaf.

In addition, you can offer a reframe, saying what your child said in the tone you would have preferred. You don't necessarily need to say, "I would have preferred if you said it like this," but you simply restate it. If, for example, your child says, "get out of my room" when you come in to check on them, perhaps you would restate it in this way: "It sounds like you think this is a bad time or you would like some space. Got it." You can turn and leave before you get into a back-and-forth, even if your child makes a comment as you go.

Your child may respond with the same attitude, "Duh, that's why I said to get out!" To which you can say, if you think it is necessary, "Ok, I was just restating it in a way that came across kindly, which I hope you keep practicing." You could also use this reframing approach later in the day and not feel the pressure of having to respond and reframe in the moment. "Hey, earlier when I came in your room, you clearly didn't want me there when you told me to get out. Next time, I would like you to find a kinder way to let me know you need some space."

Tone is a constant struggle in family dynamics, some-times driven by the parents and sometimes driven by the kids, and it is important to be cautious about how much power you give to it. The lack of tolerance our kids have for us at this time is palpable and their tone helps them feel some power. You can help them feel in power in healthy ways through being thoughtful about the situations you feel the need to manage, monitor, nag about. There might be low- to mid-risk situations that you can step out of to see how they pan out whereas in the mid to high-level risk situations, all of which you need to define together, you might use more of your emotional currency to play an active role.

Additionally, if your child has struggles with social prag-matics, hearing and understanding their tone and the tone of others, then it will be good to come up with a plan with the treatment team on what role is important for you to play, as you might need to become more of a patient teacher to help connect the dots with your child.

Preparing to Use New Communication

So much of what we teach rests in our responses and how we communicate with others. With the foundation you have built, we share these concepts to enhance your ability to **enact** new styles of communication.

Transparency

Transparency is one of the many gifts wilderness and extended residential treatment programs utilize that we encourage you to establish within your family system. These environments offer full transparency directly in the work with students and their families. Within these treatment modalities, students learn how to hear *direct, clear,* and *sincere* feedback regarding observations being made of them, every day, all of the time. They also learn the importance of being transparent with their feelings and thoughts, encouraging *honesty* and *straightforwardness* while teaching them how to be *explicit* in their communication.

Bringing this type of transparency into your home will be the key in your ability to be successful communicators. It will also allow you the opportunity to honor your child's investment in their work as they now are more than likely capable of being able to hear and participate in direct and healthy communication. This is an unmissable opportunity for you as a parent.

The Pace at Which We Move

Many adults are fast talkers and faster at processing some information in comparison with our growing children. We can be quick to assume that we understand and are connecting all of the dots. Two things can go wrong with this... at least two. The first is miscommunication and the second is that we don't listen, truly, listen. The way we each translate situations can be different and that, along with the above stated obstacles, can cause major relationship tension.

This strain can also happen between co-parents as easily as it can between a parent and child. In general, we either have a fast processing speed where we can take in information quickly, discern it, and identify and execute next steps or it just simply takes us longer. There is no right or wrong way. It just is and the important bit is to know your speed and the speed of those around you, while remembering, it's the faster processor who needs to adjust and slow down.

In our guiding principles at the start of the book, we mention the importance of buying yourself time and being curious. We see these as the top two habits, both in the parent-child dynamic and among co-parents, that can help you **enact** new communication through the transition.

As you prepare to bring your child home, it can help everyone to be clear that you are committed to slowing things down so thoughtful decisions can be made. Your job is to break the old pattern of catering to immediate gratification and shift into prioritizing the development of delayed gratification where you can.

How do you intentionally break the habit of catering to immediate gratification? Start with curiosity. Find words that fit for you that convey the message, "Tell me more."

"I want to order new shoes, can I have your credit card?"

"Tell me about the shoes. What do you love about them? How much do they cost?" Unless the situation is so farfetched that it's a clear "no", make sure to ask questions that illustrate openness, rather than questions that put one on the defensive such as, "are you kidding me? Why do you need new shoes we just got you some?" You can show up with curiosity about why your child wants them without committing to a "yes."

In addition to your commitment to slowing things down, consider cementing that commitment through not making decisions in the moment. Giving yourself five minutes, 30 minutes, a whole day if needed, whatever it takes to buy yourself time increases your chances of making a well-thought-out decision. Being able to say to your child, "I need to think about it but will have an answer for you by tomorrow," offers a time bound follow up which sets you up for account-ability with following through. This is a good thing, as often-times, our kids don't trust us when we tell them we will think about it and get back to them. All too often, we either forget or avoid, a tendency that does not engender the trust we need to encourage our kids to keep working with us through these moments.

By **mastering** these habits, you are more able to practice your own emotional regulation and you help your children develop their brains in ways that our world does not anymore, with everything at their fingertips. If you were previously in a pattern of dropping everything to meet the last minute de-mands of your children or if you trained your children that if they pestered you enough you would give in to their requests, keep this on the lists of behaviors that you want to keep your eye on for your growth.

We encourage families to consider **enacting** a useful tool we created called the "Book of Asks" in order to help facilitate a different rhythm in response to requests. If your whole family is clear on the idea and you can lead the charge of making the Book of Asks a habit, weaving into the fabric of things, you can support the development of critical thinking. It further helps you to **enact** wise-minded decisions through prioritizing delayed gratification and you can help your children develop competency through being clear about the role they play in getting the things they want.

The Book of Asks is a notebook that lives in a common room area and is a place to write down the "I wants" when your children ask for things that are important to take time to consider. We guide families to identify essential questions to help them make thoughtful decisions such as: "what do we need to see over what period of time to get to yes on this?" and "what are the pros and cons of this?" It is a useful tool in helping you and your family form a habit of slowing down while allowing you to validate your child's interest without brushing them off. With consistency, your children will shift out of the childlike approach of demanding things "now" and the whole system will learn to tolerate and live in the practice that "now" means "no".

As with everything we teach, these are tools not rules. It is important to predict the situations that are most important for the Book of Asks and situations that you might figure out more on the fly. For some, it might be items above a certain monetary value or situations that carry more risk. And, if your child has just been bad mouthing you or refusing to help around the house, you have our permission to just say no, without curiosity or validating or any of those compassionate skills you have been practicing. Sometimes an eye roll by a parent followed by, "are you kidding me?" is simply the best response.

 **Nugget of Knowledge:** As you're trying on these news skills and language, it is not uncommon for your child to say that you sound like a therapist. Claim it and say, "well, that is because I learned this through therapy and the work I am doing, and I think it is important."

Building Reassurance in Your Co-Parenting Team

Throughout this journey with a child in treatment, it is likely that one of you has applied more time toward reading, letter writing, and following through with homework from the program. There is often one primary voice leading the charge and the other parent fills in a line or two from their perspective or gets the cliffs notes from the parent who read the whole book in two days. It is important to recognize if there is resentment around this and how that resentment is expressed, because it will continue to come out with your child(ren).

The fact is that parents, just like the rest of the humans out there, have different strengths, ways of understanding things, and skills. They also have things they tend to avoid for a myriad of reasons. Accepting this reality and being clear about your roles is important. To do this, you must be willing to talk about it first. The more you can acknowledge and address the dynamics of your co-parenting relationship while your child is in treatment the better. Understanding what the roles in the co-parenting team have been and how they need to change moving forward will allow you to focus and rely on your strengths as a co-parenting team.

As you will not be able to address, discuss, and resolve every co-parenting dynamic that will play out before your child comes home, it will be helpful to identify how and where you will continue to have these conversations, bringing resolution and change. The approach is twofold – first, have times and places where you protect yourselves from talking about the kids. Maybe this is in the bedroom before bed or any time after 10pm. You need to know that, unless there is a true emergency, which you can define in advance, these times and places are safe from having to think about and talk through it.

We suspect your life needs time for things other than working through parenting challenges. Secondly, carve out dedicated, consistent time to focus on parenting matters which should include setting a time limit. This could be 30 minutes while in a park, out to lunch or even over the phone. Consider the idea of keeping it organized, each coming with one or two urgent/important situations or themes that truly feel worth your time and emotional currency. The topics, for example, could include talking about how a situation went in the week and brainstorming other ways to manage it if it happens again or it could be predicting something coming up that you want to be prepared for.

If you need to be more spontaneous about it due to unforeseen circumstances that have interfered with your consistent, focused time, make sure to check in with each other before you start unloading to ensure that you both have the bandwidth. If one of you does not then make a commitment to talk within a short, agreed-upon time, regardless of your bandwidth, so things do not build up.

Even with a commitment to discuss certain situations before a decision is made, there will be times when one parent or the other needs to or chooses to "parent on the fly". To parent on the fly well, a few skills are required of the co-parenting team. Reassurance and trust stand out as the most vital necessities to be able to give each other permission, which is essential to make a unilateral decision in the moment.

In your commitment to dig deep and talk through the strengths and weaknesses of your co-parenting you may come to find out that trust has been impacted along the way, you may come to find that you, as the other co-parent, were not as reliable as you thought. A great way to gain trust in allowing for one parent to be able to "parent on the fly" is to build on experiences that provide reliability and reassurance. The more a co-parent shows their reliability by doing what they say they will do, the more reassurance there will be, and the more trust is built and restored.

It is further essential to honor each other's uniqueness. You were individuals with separate opinions prior to parenting and that is likely what brought you together. Honor that you do not need to do things exactly the same way in order to be effective people and parents. That none of us is always right and different approaches work with different kids at different times and for different reasons. Remembering this will allow each parent to have grace and awareness that sometimes solo parenting decisions will go well and align with each parent's perspective and sometimes it will not. It will most likely be okay if the opportunity for grace and recovery are granted.

Often in a co-parenting team, parents who function from opposite ends of the spectrum tend to further polarize each other as they try to compensate for the other's approach. While working to get on the same page in terms of a situation regarding their child, we encourage parents to **enact** the "connect then redirect" approach. If one of you has strengths with redirecting, then put more focus on connecting first and vice versa, if one tends to connect and leave out the redirect, then put focus on adding redirecting to your approach. This can help co-parents witness growth in each other, which builds reassurance, which builds more trust and shows commitment while accepting that neither way is the "right" way all of the time.

Dedication, focus, and consistency are what it takes to make changes in general. Finding ways to incorporate these attributes in your parenting will go a long way, especially in your co-parenting relationship. Being reliable in your co-parenting relationship will establish and increase long-term reassurance and trust. In many ways, this is where you will find yourselves on the same playing field as your child. As you move forward and witness yourself being overwhelmed by emotion, struggling with consistency, and forgetting your skills when you are face-to-face with a challenging moment, use that to lean into empathy and patience as you recognize how hard it will be for your child to **enact** their new skills.

Remember. Reflect. Revisit.

- Before you bring a child home from treatment, predict and prepare for the top three to five situations you are likely to face in the first month.
- Watch out for the traps – your kids play a role by setting them, but it is on you to notice and avoid them.
- Use your healthy communication skills to solidify the co-parenting team.

Home Agreements: Identifying & Enacting What Matters

Now it is time to put it all into action and be guided into more specifics surrounding the actual transition home. Within a transition home, the first 90 days are crucial as it's enough time to allow for change, regression, relapse, continued growth, redirection, and recovery.

This is where you will earn trust that you mean what you say, that you can approach things wise-mindedly, and that you are reliable as a parent.

This is where you will observe the old patterns as well as the new ones so that you can shape your lives and your family system using current and accurate data.

This is where you will learn how to implement borrowed concepts and see which work and which do not.

This is where you will be challenged to see how effective your home plan truly can be.

This is where remembering that being committed to habits and processes for yourself is more important than having the perfect set of rules, privileges, or consequences for your child.

In the process of transition and choosing the guardrails you want to put into place to help your child stay on track, you will set yourself up for success if you are realistic with what *you* can and cannot follow through with. For example, if you say that your adolescent can't go in their bedroom except to sleep the first two months they are home because you are concerned about old patterns of isolation and self-harm, understand that there are eight weeks' worth of challenging moments you need to be prepared for as your child pushes against this each week.

Identifying ahead of time what is important to you about that kind of rule and whether it's really a set up for success is key to *your* success. You are likely to be in situations where you find exceptions to that rule and as such don't follow it. While in general we push toward consistency rather than rigidity, it can be better to not set something up from the start that will require lots of exceptions.

Power in the Parenting

First and foremost, as you embark on the process of creating a home agreement, it's imperative that you under-stand where the true power is. The power in home agreements is in your parenting, not in the piece of paper. Sit with that for a minute; let that marinate. We stress the enormity of this statement frequently when supporting parents during the transition home.

Parents regularly talk about putting the home agreement on the fridge to remind their child about what they agreed to, having something to point to when there are struggles. While it is important for your child to see and understand your home and parenting expectations, we encourage parents to consider what we see as more important, which is that the home agreement be viewed as a commitment between parents first. View it as a handshake deal if you will, about what *your* commitments are to guide and respond to the ups and downs, what you do and don't support, and what changes you will be making as parents.

It is often, though not always, recommended that your child play an integral role in the development of the home agreement. Knowing your child's commitments to themselves provides a great source of data for you as a parent. Typically, when parents ask their child while they are still in treatment what commitments they have for themselves, a genuine response is given. However, it is important for parents to know that they need to follow through with their part, even when your child's commitment wanes once home.

Given that it is truly a commitment from the parents to guide and respond in the ways they say they will, if the home agreement does not fully and truly fit you as a parent, then it will not be a successful resource for you and will end up being a piece of paper you wave around in desperation, wondering why it's not working. For some, it will be the scapegoat to prove nothing is working while too easily ignoring the fact that you as the parent are the one who created it and are in charge of implementing it.

Our stance on where the power lies is not meant to discount the useful intentions behind constructing a home agreement. Rather, it means that you need to engage in its creation as a parent who is committed to looking at themselves first, a parent who is committed to understanding where you are and where you want to be while being realistic about your own capability in the implementation of your end of the agreement. Additionally, this process also includes you as a parent not putting your child in a place of potentially feeling disempowered or oppressed. You can avoid this by identifying where you can transfer the responsibility to them by seeking out knowledge on where their commitments to themselves lie.

For every category you believe you need to have expectations in, ask your child where his commitments are to himself in those areas and what he believes he needs from you or other resources to help him follow through with those commitments. Asking your child these questions as you are preparing your home agreement gives you much needed data and it empowers your child and gives him a voice. This data also gives you knowledge as to how quickly you can transfer responsibility and in what areas. In some areas it can be given immediately and sometimes it's a transfer of responsibility that goes slowly over time.

Exercise

My Expectation	How will I measure and monitor if it's being followed?	My options of a response if the expectation is not met.
Our expectation is that you have no missing school assignments.	We will look at the portal every Wednesday evening and Friday after school.	If there are missing assignments, you have Thursday and Friday to complete them and work issues out with your teachers **(transfer of responsibility)** If they are

		still missing on Friday you will lose specific weekend privileges to create space to complete missing assignments before the new school week.
The expectation is that you give to the household by taking the garbage out on garbage night by 8pm.	*We will know you took it out because you will let us know that you have completed it (transfer of responsibility).*	*If you don't let us know, we will most likely still check and if it's not out by garbage night at 8pm you will lose a specific privilege though you will have a chance to try again the next week. (Ex. decrease in weekend spending money that is parent provided, loss of gaming for one weekend night)*

Your turn...

When we work with parents who are in the process of determining the guardrails they want to put into place to help their child stay on the path toward thriving, we lead with this concept that a home agreement truly is an agreement among parents. Again, the commitment is between parents as they identify where they want to parent, how they want to parent, the expectations they want to have and how they will respond when their child doesn't always follow through.

We see parents as more developmentally capable of following through. While you might collaborate with your child to identify healthy habits and unhealthy habits as well as expectations, privileges and consequences, parents developmentally are more capable of living true to their agreements and commitments than is their child.

There are many amazing, powerful, and life-changing approaches and interventions that are used in wilderness therapy and extended residential treatment. However, it's important to remember we can't duplicate these treatment methods, but we can borrow from the concepts and tweak them so they fit your family system. The trick is understanding from where and what you can borrow and what your ability as a parent and a family system is to implement the tweaked concept. If the home agreement doesn't fit you first as a parent, then the expectation of your child being able to follow it will bring great frustration and disappointment.

"Travis just got home and we tried to sit down to review the home agreement again and he said that he just agreed to it to get out of treatment and that he does not plan to follow it. What do we do?"

First, it is important to be aware of the trap that many parents fall into, presuming that the child is always being manipulative. Sometimes they are and sometimes they are not and if you can react as though you believe they are not being manipulative, you can still hold your boundary while shifting the tone of your response. An opportunist is defined as a person who exploits circumstances to gain immediate advantage rather than being guided by consistent principles or plans. That sounds like the definition of how most kids work. Setting yourself up for success is reminding yourself of the normalcy in your child's behavior, the importance of addressing the undesirable behavior and expecting a kid to be a kid.

We have worked with students in wilderness programs who wholeheartedly believe in their ability to live within the expected parameters but who, once home, are overtaken by waves of temptation – with friends, technology, and more and their perseverance submits to the impulsive desires. This is developmentally appropriate and is exactly why we remind parents that the power is in their parenting and not the piece of paper. In moments like these, when kids are appropriately being opportunists, they are reliant on their parents to help them determine if this approach they are attempting, will or will not work for them to achieve what they want.

In Travis' case, which happens often, we encourage parents first to remember where the power is, in that moment when the "piece of paper" is in front of them. When you remember the power is in you, in your parenting, consider saying, "well, that is understandable, and we hear that you are saying you are not committed to this and maybe you're not ready for us to fully take you for your word. We are going to stick with ours and follow this agreement and if you want to connect and collaborate with us in the weeks to come, let us know."

Keep in mind that your child would like for some things to go back the way they were, when they would dig their heels in, and the rules would change because at one time in your family's dynamic, this was an effective tool for them. Since you're committed to changing this pattern, this is a great opportunity to do just that, prove to your child that things are changing and encouraging them to adapt.

Nugget of Knowledge: Just because a strategy sounds good on paper doesn't mean it will fit your style or your family. Knowing this will assist you in creating an authentic home agreement that fits you as a parent first.

Grounding Your Expectations

Our guiding principles proposed the following questions as we addressed developmental stages: *Are we expecting too much or too little? Are they truly capable of following through*

194

with a commitment during certain developmental stages? If we understood developmental stages, would we really be so surprised at what our kids do or say? This is where these questions come back into play as you identify what your expectations of your child are.

Let's dive in and start talking about one of the first things treatment teams often guide parents through during the process of creating home agreements, which is identifying the non-negotiables. Non-negotiables are the lines parents are not willing to allow their child to cross. We have seen many non-negotiables, from lying to illustrating a pattern of substance abuse. It is a prerequisite that parents define what non-negotiable means to them. Sometimes it means that that a behavior or choice will not be tolerated, and that behavior is non-negotiable.

If that example resonates with you, what does that mean? What exactly does not tolerated mean to you? How do you convey "not tolerated"? If something is truly non-negotiable, what happens when the behavior occurs? Perhaps it is a pattern of high-risk behavior that is truly non-negotiable but the steps before a situation gets to that point is where you are willing to work through with your child. If the response is anything other than being asked to leave the home or go back to treatment, then it maybe actually negotiable.

Your consequence to any of the behaviors that are not helping your child thrive can certainly be non-negotiable but the act of being involved in the behavior is theirs to choose and more than likely out of your control. Substance use and abuse is a common high-risk behavior and a significant area of concern for many parents in transition. With this framework, you can have non-negotiable guardrails, for example, drug testing. You can say that engaging in random drug testing for the first six months is non-negotiable and that, if your child refuses the test, you will count it as positive and there will be consequences that you will implement which may include engaging more treatment. Non-negotiables have a similar feel to trying to put a boundary *onto* someone. Like boundaries, the art of non-negotiables is to be clear that it's *your* non-negotiable and allow your child to accept and adjust to it.

This is part of your continued work, to ground yourself in your expectations by being realistic and finding stability in your parenting decisions. To help with this, we want to share one of our beliefs. One of the greatest skills kids who go to treatment acquire is the skill of adapting and adjusting to ideas, rules, and people that they don't like or agree with. Kids who go to treatment start the practice of this crucial life skill within minutes of the process starting. Our encouragement for you as a parent is to capitalize on it and remind yourselves over and over that no matter what changes your child did or did not make during her time in treatment, it's as close to a guarantee that we can get, that she has the skill to accept and adjust to things she does not like or agree with – which includes you and your parenting.

 **Nugget of Knowledge:** In general, negotiation is a great skillset and, in a parent-child relationship, the only way a negotiation really happens is when a parent invites it. Kids will appropriately attempt to negotiate, but it's a parent who invites the negotiation. Parents **honing** in on what it really means for them to say it's non-negotiable is key.

Set Up for Success & Own What You Are Offering

Clearly, we cannot say enough, as here we are saying it again, about how important it is that you set yourselves up for success. Part of this is knowing what you are setting yourself up for when it comes to being the "step-down" from your child's treatment experience. You, your home, and your community are now the next step in your child's treatment process. Leaving treatment is not an end, it's leaving a higher level of therapeutic support to move into the next phase that will focus on sustaining the therapeutic work.

We often discuss what we call the container effect of wilderness or long term residential treatment. These treatment milieus do a tremendous job of containing anxiety, substance use, depression, and attentional issues, just to name a few. As transition experts, we are constantly examining the loss of the container effect and addressing the impact it has on the transition. This also includes strategizing how to create a parent version of the container in the home environment and recognizing you will not be able to provide the same container.

Therapeutic environments have the ability to establish thoughtful control over day-to-day rhythms, the social milieu or even getting your child to engage in ongoing therapeutic support. In treatment, if you don't go to therapy, therapy comes to you and if you are not engaging authentically, there is a safe environment that embraces you until you are ready. At home, you can show up for your weekly session and then head back into the world of temptation.

We don't share this to make you feel hopeless about the possibility of success at home but rather to offer clarity about the reality of the situation and to impress upon you the importance of ongoing assessment, planning and reviewing as you face varying situations without the ability to control the container as much. Your guardrails, which are there to help your children understand the consequences of the choices they make and how you will respond, contribute to the safety of the container. Additionally, when a child comes home, it is so that they can thrive *at home,* which includes the reality of the looseness of the container.

As you go through this process of preparing your home container and creating your home agreements, it's crucial that you as parents **own** what you are offering and more importantly what you are not. Establishing that clarity is one of the easiest ways to identify your boundaries. Are you offering the opportunity to stay out past midnight or are you not? Are you offering to provide access to a car as soon as they return home or are you not? Your role is to stand strong in your offerings while you wait for your child with their newfound skills, to accept and adjust to your offerings even when they don't like it or like you for it.

Standing strong in your offerings, or more importantly in what you are not offering, requires the crucial skill of tolerating the discomfort of saying no. What doesn't work is using statements that share your discomfort like, "I am un-comfortable with you staying out past midnight," or, "I am uncomfortable with the outfit you are wearing". This is not a phrase of ownership; it's a phrase of discomfort and it invites negotiation from your child with the intention of encouraging you to get comfortable in allowing them to do what they want.

Using this approach also implies that you as a parent are relying on your child to do or say something to make *you* more comfortable, to ease your discomfort. This is not their responsibility. Statements like, "I am willing," or, "I am not will-ing," "I am open to you doing this," and, "I am not open to you doing that," "I am offering to provide that," and, "I am not offering to give you this" are all approaches that will instill the **ownership** for your parenting decisions.

 **Nugget of Knowledge:** It is your responsibility as parents to create the container that best fits your child at this time and **own** the guardrails or scaffolding that you put into place.

Use of Templates & Other Transition Resources

In addition to having clarity and **ownership**, a primary piece of setting yourselves up for success, as you know, includes being in agreement as parents. To ensure you can get to this place, we believe going through the process of creating home agreement drafts will be of great assistance and to your advantage. And this much needed process can often be hijacked by the use of standard templates when creating a home agreement. Many parents will seek out and receive a template or outline to use to support the process of creating structure at home and we want to take a stance on the use of templates.

Templates can be useful to help parents stir creative juices. Rather than having a blank canvas that they need to construct on their own, having guidelines can save a lot of frustration. However, it is important to not become overly dependent on a template, as it can lead you into a structure that is unnecessary or not doable for your unique home. Every family is unique in their values and lifestyle and, given the stress of preparing for transition, you can lose the uniqueness of your family by depending too much on a template for creating your home structure.

Think about a home agreement as something that can outline the healthy habits you hope to see or that you expect. Additionally, be clear about the support you will need to offer to help with those habits and privileges as you are the one that has the capability and willingness to follow through on your

199

end of the bargain. And that means that your expectations are clear, measurable, achievable and observable. Telling your child that they cannot watch TV during the day until homework is done and then having them home alone for hours does not set this expectation up for success. Instead, it sets you up to play detective and for them to lie because developmentally, it is unlikely they are ready to manage technology and screens wholly on their own.

For those of you who grew up latchkey kids, you know what it was like listening for the garage to open or car to pull into the driveway so that you could shut off MTV and run back to your room to make it look like you had been doing your homework the whole time. Instead, make your expectations measurable and observable by being clear on the expectations of homework being turned in and grades being at a certain level and set technology limits that you can control.

We have created a free transition resource that guides families through many of the questions that we are suggesting you consider in this transition-focused portion of H.O.M.E. It includes suggestions of categories, such as Academics, Physical Health, Family Time, under which parents can define their expectations and identify the guardrails needed to help their children meet those expectations. It also encourages you to identify your hopes in each area so you are clear on your ability to distinguish between hopes and expectations which allows you to be clear on what is in your control. The questions and exercises in our transition resource can help you get clear with aspects that you might want to fit into any template that you find or a program uses to support this process.

Use this QR code to locate your free transition resource.

Friends & Foes: Finding Your Tribe

Home is much bigger than just the family unit when it comes to the social lives of children. Connection and acceptance in peer relationships are a part of our basic needs, especially in adolescence. Finding their way to identify healthy connections and friendships that are authentic while minimizing the risk that can come with adolescent peer relationships is a part of their developmental journey, as it was yours at one time.

Hopefully the guidance in Part 1 regarding the importance of finding your community stirred you to shape your support network. While there are great online support groups, it is also imperative to have a community of family or friends who know your true story, who hold it in confidence and who can be there for your whole family in whatever ways you need. One avenue is through reengaging with hobbies, or starting a new one, and finding a group that you can join. This resolves some of the need for healthy routines, gets your focus on something other than your family and helps you to develop community. This is an area that is worth investing time in and, as you assess your emotional currency, could take the place of something that drains more than it replenishes.

Your child has also spent time in treatment working to understand who their tribe is at home, identifying the friends that help them to set a low bar and the friends who might be more willing to encourage them to be their best self. Creating a healthy social life outside of treatment can be daunting, depending on the life your child was living prior to treatment. After being gone, peer groups will have reformed and changed and even old healthy groups might be hard to get back into. Unfortunately, it may be easier to get reinvolved with some of the not so healthy friends. Even though parents should have expectations about peer relationships and connections, the reality is you can only know and control so much.

When your child walks out the door, you will not have control over how and with whom your child interacts. However, you can spend time coaching your child on how to identify and navigate risky friendships, those defined as the ones that may not serve them and potentially put them in risky situations, including that of regression and relapse. You can also prioritize your energy and expectations by insisting that your child join a club or even get a part time volunteer or paying job.

Curiosity is key as you try to understand your child's social skill set, or lack thereof. Perhaps through the treatment process you learned that your daughter misses some social cues, mistranslates things, or reacts sensitively to interactions that to you seem mundane. Perhaps you learned that she does better one-on-one than in a group or is more confident with people who are more mature than maybe with people her own age. Gaining clarity in some of these areas can support the collaboration process with your child as you shape expectations around non-digital social interactions. If this continues to be a struggle area, make sure that it is a topic that the therapist at home is ready to address. Keep in mind that your child does not need a group of 10 to be stable and sometimes just one or two constant companions is enough.

Perhaps you are using the language of red, yellow, and green light friends to determine a path to support a healthy social life upon your child's return. A memorable experience in our time as wilderness therapists was when the list of appropriate peers was being determined and parents believed they were confident on what category certain peers fell in. Upon seeing the list, kids would often respond with, "Wow, my mom thinks Joe is a green light friend, I smoked a ton with Joe the day before I came here." And, often the opposite, a peer who may have a reputation that is undesirable for you, may be the friend who encourages your child to be their best self.

While this is an effective tool in allowing everyone to be a part of the process to understand who are friends, who are foes and who lie somewhere in the middle, it is also important to keep in mind that your child *is a* green, yellow or red friend in someone else's parents' eyes. Just like you might want your child to be given another chance by them, consider which friends on your list you might be willing to get to know better by having them over to your house or inviting them out to dinner once your child is home. It might be some time before you are comfortable with them being on their own together, but what effort might you be willing to extend?

Similar to enforcing a slow reintroduction to electronics in their lives, we encourage a thoughtful, tiered approach to bringing peers back into the picture. For some, specifically those who tended to isolate, we suggest that parents have in-person interactions as a requirement for earning some privileges. For children who had unhealthy and perhaps reckless relationships, we guide parents to require some at home interactions with friends first. Parents can get an eye on how they interact with each other, without hawking over them. You can set expectations such as that they pick up after themselves, perhaps even asking them to help with preparing and making dinner or with baking a desert that everyone can enjoy.

Then, you can move into allowing for peer connections away from home, with clear curfew and a planned activity like a movie before you move into more flexible and less restrictive peer connections. Throughout this process, you can be clear with your child that, over time, while you still hope they can make healthy friend choices, that they are responsible for their own actions, regardless of who they decide to hang out with. With this focus, you can note that healthy decisions in other areas of life such as with school or choosing what they need to do over what they want to do, can help them to earn the trust that they can make healthy decisions when out with friends.

An unexpected challenge through this transition is how your child might experience grief over loss of peer community and the constant connection while in treatment. One of the benefits of therapeutic program life is the nature of the peer group. On one hand, you have a group of struggling adolescents or young adults together in one place where unhealthy habits can be communicated and shared, just like in the real world. On the other hand, they are mostly all working toward something better, both scenarios with a therapeutic team to support them working through it. Often-times "cool" gets redefined as being able to take account-ability, or practicing healthy coping, which can be hard to find in the real world of teen and Young Adult (YA) living.

While we are sure it was not all smooth sailing and they probably complained about some of the peers they were with, they also made connections, had positive experiences, were mentees and mentors, and probably were the most vulnerable they have been in their lives. There is also a social simplicity to this environment which is constant companionship; someone always around to chat it up with, someone to entertain or be entertained by during times of perceived boredom.

Just as they were plopped into treatment suddenly, at least from their perspective, the transition out can often be sudden and compound a sense of loss and loneliness. As peer relationships at home are renegotiated and limitations are put into place, you may see them struggle navigating this loneliness. Attune to what is happening and be cautious that it doesn't compel you to loosen your established boundaries and rules around peer relationships sooner than you might have.

"Alyssa seems so lonely. She wants to Snapchat with a few of the girls from wilderness, but we said we were going to wait until she had a couple weeks of school under her belt before we opened up social media. We want her to have a foundation of a healthy rhythm before the metaphorical flood gates open that distract her from healthy living. She also asked to go out with a group of girls, some are yellow friends, and some are green, to a party. She has only been home for a week, but she is making it clear that it is our fault she is lonely and in her room all the time. What do we do?"

With this and other common situations of pushback that you will face, it is important that parents commit to a process to make thoughtful, wise-minded co-parenting decisions. Identifying essential questions to check in and remind yourself as to why you have implemented a rule or expectation can be helpful, such as:

- What compelled you to have this rule in the first place?
- It was important to you two weeks ago before she was home. Has the intention of it or value behind the situation changed?
- If you stick to your decision and say no, do you feel confident in handling the potential fall out, which could also earn you trust that you do actually mean what you say?
- What are the pros and cons of changing your decision and saying yes?
- What might you need to see from her to get to yes?
- Do you think she is capable of handling loneliness, following rules to invite friends to the house in order to have social engagement to stave off that

loneliness, or do you need to change your rules to make it more tolerable for her because of her fragility? And, will it help her be less fragile?

- Are there other solutions, such as encouraging her to get the job that you all agreed she would get?

Prior to a child leaving treatment, we encourage parents to ask them to identify a few healthy peers and adults with whom they are willing to share their story and to ask them to be part of their support network. This could include writing a letter about what the norm was prior to treatment, what they have learned, what they hope for their future and what support they might need. We also encourage that the support network come together in the first week of them being home to solidify the connection and security. Their treatment team might also have other approaches to facilitating something similar and parents can steward this forward, for themselves and for their children.

 **Nugget of Knowledge:** Peer groups and relationships are one of the most difficult transitions to navigate. Your best approach is to be clear about how you will implement your expectations and how you will respond when it becomes clear just how difficult it is for everyone.

Finding Your Rhythm to Assess, Plan, & Review

Many parents find it helpful to commit to a review process, inviting themselves and their child to engage in dialogue throughout the transition process to check in, specifically about what is going well and identify areas that need extra attention. Creating platforms to highlight the strengths and to discuss desired changes is often encouraged and this can be easily identified as daily check-ins and family meetings.

This is a great example of borrowing from a concept that works in treatment while acknowledging the importance of tweaking it so it fits for your family. The phrase "check-in" is common language within wilderness and oftentimes extended into residential settings. To be able to "check-in" is an opp-ortunity that these modalities offer students to share their concerns, feelings, proud moments, and feedback they may want to give. Sometimes they are spontaneous and some-times they are before or after a planned group. For parents, it's important to remember you are not the group they left, nor can you replicate the version of the staff member that helped facilitate these moments. What you are is their parent and family system who wants to incorporate the idea of "checking-in" by making the concept yours.

Ideally, throughout your day-to-day parenting you will be "checking in" by participating in moments of connection with your child, by sharing your feelings and thoughts that you are experiencing in the moment and encouraging them to share theirs. Being in the mindset of being a parent who "takes notice" is also highlighted in these moments as well as in more formal family meetings. Taking notice means you are aware of your child's behaviors, actions, and comments both good and bad. You're willing to also take notice as to how you are doing and how you are feeling.

If you live in this mindset, then you will be able to engage in sharing your concerns as well as giving affirmations in consistent daily interactions. This concept can be really helpful during the honeymoon phase of the transition, during which it seems your child is doing almost everything "right". Use this time as an opportunity to intentionally identify and write down all the skills you see him using, noting his ability to transfer what he learned in treatment to home.

When the honeymoon phase starts to wane, you will have this knowledge to remind you of the abilities he has. The hope is that you can then regulate your reactions with the belief that he has learned something and that it is hard to put into action consistently over time, rather than reacting with the belief that all is lost. This further encourages you to address the behavior in front of you as an incident and not see it as the upheaval of the transition.

Finding your rhythm as a family can include consistent family meetings, your family's process of assessing and reviewing, anything that offers everyone in the system an opportunity to participate and to learn and practice new styles of communication and engagement. We encourage you to really spend time identifying in advance what this could look like for you as parents, what you want to get out of it, where you can collaborate with your children to hear what they might consider getting out of it and identifying the best way for you to implement it.

We encourage family meetings to be a place for discussion that allows everyone to have a voice in regards to how they think or feel the family is doing. It is a place to address any concerns as well as a place where you process through any changes that are being requested or that you want to consider making. When it is clear that this is where requests for changes can be made it allows you to be more prepared when your child pushes for changes on day two of being home or when you as parents believe things are going so well one week into the transition that you are feeling compelled to make a change.

With this type of planning, you can commit to sticking with "what is" for a period of time, and then reviewing thoughtfully on a schedule. This is a strategy that keeps you as a parent from celebrating too early and from making emotional decisions. It encourages a wise-minded process that includes collaboration and critical thinking and allows you to truly establish a healthy rhythm of being home.

Nugget of Knowledge: Asking your child ten times a day, "how are you feeling?" is not the role you want to play when **enacting** your version of "check-ins".

Consistency

As we have said, there are predictable situations you can create a plan for in advance, so you feel prepared to deliver a consistent and reliable response. However, if parents are frequently responding to situations in opposing ways, the intermittent nature of the response to the disoriented ping and the unpredictability of parents can lead to confusion, lack of trust and ultimately lack of safety. Many children, with their emotional and behavioral responses, need to be contained when they cannot contain themselves and the consistency and predictability of your responses can lend to that security.

Another reason to get parents on the same page is that predictability and consistency can help to shape behavior and choices. Just as the disoriented child needs a clear and consistent response to help them find their path, consistency with responses between parents is key to shaping the tone of the home. As parents, you can have different personalities, different styles of engagement, even different relationships with your children *and* you can still be consistent in your parenting positions and your responses to them.

Adolescents are gifted with the powerful skill to engage in the debate as if they were the lawyer, the judge, the defense attorney, the prosecutor, and the jury *all* within the same conversation. It's a skill parents once had during their adolescentyears that has been appropriately lost because as adults, we don't often keep relationships where this type of engagement is needed to meet our wants and needs. It's also important to remember that adolescents are not good at distinguishing between wants and needs and, in general, see everything as a need. So, instead of trying to respond to each role your child is playing to get their needs and wants, be consistent with your one response and hit repeat.

Applying Tools with Success: Lisa's experience.

One of our favorite parent reports of success in executing one of our strategies is when Lisa, the mom of a 16-year-old boy, told us that her son was out and about and excessively texting her trying to get one of his "needs" met. She told us that by having the opportunity to take space, since they were texting, she decided she was going to cut and paste her response, the texting version of "hit repeat".

As her son kept responding, she was able to more clearly see how he was able to jump around in the roles we described. Lisa said the best part of the communication process was when, after a dozen or so cut and paste responses, her son finally responded with, "Mom why do you keep saying the exact same thing?" and she was able to say, "because you keep asking the same question, just in different ways."

Enacting these processes and knowing how, when, and why to use them, can get you through many experiences in new ways. While they might seem like old behaviors or situations you wished you would not be in again, you get to help redefine them through your new responses. Also, the more you solidify the foundation of your relationship through **mastery**, the better you all will recover after managing some of the higher risk situations, such as addictive behaviors.

Addictive Behaviors: Electronics & Substance Use

While we are not going to outline each possible obstacle for which you might want to set an expectation, we would like to focus on a few sensitive areas like electronics, substance use, and managing potentially addictive behaviors. Remember the container effect in treatment we spoke about? When it comes to addictive behaviors, the therapeutic environment contained accessibility, impulse control, excessive consumption, and choice making. As you now know, it's your role and responsibility to create the home environment version of this container that includes prioritizing abstinence where necessary and balanced living where appropriate.

Electronics

Throw all your electronics out the window for the first year after your child transitions home.

Electronics... actually.

Ok, now that we got that fantasy out of the way, we can talk about ideas on how to *actually* manage the reality of screens at home, which tends to be one of the biggest points of contention for most families. Many parents we work with often comment on the need for a phone in their child's life for convenience of communication and awareness of their location. This simple and often appropriate need parents have is complicated by the device being a phone, mini-computer, and gaming console all in one. This is an area where you as a parent can focus your attention first on **owning** what you are offering and then focusing on the parameters you need to put around what you are providing.

Your child has experienced abstinence through their time in treatment and, if in a longer-term treatment, perhaps started to slowly reintegrate it into life. Regardless of their technology use in treatment, it is important that parents continue to set parameters. Identifying parameters is based on several factors and many can be determined by examining your child's possible unhealthy use of devices, your values as parents, ages of your children, and the values you are instilling around healthy device use for the family as a whole.

Further, as your children make arguments about the problem solving and teamwork skills they are enhancing through the games they are playing, after being curious and hearing more about it, you can also initiate a conversation about how they are doing those things offline. At times, we encourage parents to work with their children to identify the benefits the kids see in being plugged in to games, YouTube, or social media and then to set weekly goals to bring those benefits into their lives without the use of screens.

Below are some common obstacles and related strategies for managing screens at home.

Prioritizing Balanced Living

More often than not, engaging in social media and playing video games is not what is "bad." It's the length of time investing in these activities, as well as immersing themselves in them without willingness to re-engage in the 4D world around them, that create problems and unhealthy patterns. We like to think about it in relation to proficiency – the more time we invest in something, the more proficient we can become. The more time you, as a parent, allow your child to game or be on social media, the more proficient you are encouraging them to be at it, and the less proficient in the world that is around them.

Prioritizing balanced living is the key and how you incorporate that into your family system is your job as a parent. Part of being able to do this will include you investing your time to become proficient, to stop claiming ignorance or age, and learning how to set up electronic monitoring through the different parent controls that are available. There are apps you can purchase and software that is built into many phones that allow you to limit the time spent in certain apps, limit accessibility to content, and give you information as to how they are spending their time when on their devices. It is always recommended that you use the paid versions of these software, otherwise your personal information is not as protected.

Your commitment to having expectations and setting up monitoring and controls allows you to use guardrails as needed, engage in moments of teaching, and redirect your child as needed around the productive and distracting time spent on their device. This will also allow you to spend your emotional currency on getting your child to engage in other productive activities because you were able to use parenting tools and controls to manage the all-too-consuming time spent on devices.

It's clear that kids are skilled at finding ways around the apps and software that are set up. This is a great time for you to keep the "let's keep trying attitude" as you invest in keeping up with the complexities of all that is available to them and remembering that kids are opportunists, so of course they are going to try. It's just more reason to invest in balanced living and to not solely focus on those supportive tools. It is also important that parents offer alternative activities for children to choose, including having game night together or with friends. Your child will push back against this initially, and we have found that when it is set up as a requirement in order to have technology time, they can adapt and get into it more than you may anticipate.

Owning What You Offer: Todd's experience.

Todd, a parent we supported through his child's transition home from treatment, decided to make a list of what he wanted his kids, especially his son who was coming out of treatment, to hear about what he was offering and what he expected when it came to phone use. He had a great way of **owning** what he was offering, being clear about his willingness to parent in this area, and attempting to influence his son on balance in our technology-filled world.

"It is my phone. I bought it. I paid for it. I am loaning it to you. Keep your eyes up. See the world happening around you. Stare out a window. Listen to the birds. Make human contact with the person sitting next to you. Wonder without googling. Do not use this technology to lie, fool, or deceive another human being. Do not involve yourself in exchanges that are hurtful to others. Be a good friend first, stay out of the drama and crossfire. Do not text, email, or say anything through this device you would not say in person. You will mess up. I will monitor and take away your phone at times. We will sit down and talk about it. We will start over again. You and I, we are always learning. I am on your team. We are in this together."

We encourage parents to have times, such as family dinner or other activities, when you ask kids to be off their phones. You can guide this based on your values and lifestyle. Further, we encourage parents to consider doing their own research on the impact of excessive screen time and technology use that impacts all of us, not just our children. Really, as a fully developed adult, honestly ask yourself how hard at times it is for you to disconnect from the scrolling loop of social media, shopping, online articles, and just daily news. We ask you as parents to be open to assessing your own screen-related activities and the importance of modeling the ability to unwind without it.

Shutting Down at Night

We agree with brain science experts that the most important screen-related situation to manage is preserving a healthy sleep routine. There is extensive evidence surrounding the importance of "shutting-down" from all devices at night to allow the body's natural sleep hormones to do their job. Again, this is an area to research and consider incorporating for you, your child, and the whole family system. You can only manage what you can monitor, so for those of you who allow devices in bedrooms, you will have to find a way to ensure the actual "shutting-down" is happening.

This is also a great time to not take the all-too-common bait, "I have homework to do, and my homework is on my computer." We know that most kids who are plugged in "doing homework" are not managing time well as they bop around the internet. So, even if your child says they need it for homework, you can make your expectation clear and brainstorm with them other ways to manage their time so that they can get all their work done by the time the "shut down" hour arrives. Remember your opportunist; if you give him the opportunity, he will take it.

Another reason we support the forced shut down and devices left out of bedrooms at night is again around a child's developmental ability to disconnect on their own without the support of parents and guardrails. We collaborated with a psychologist years ago and his message still stands out to us. He polled the adolescent clients of his shared private practice, asking this basic question, "if you had to choose between losing your ability to have access to your phone at night or to lose a vital organ which would you pick?" He reported the majority of the adolescents chose the vital organ.

As we know, one of our basic needs is acceptance (and vital organs) and for an adolescent, this is a priority even at two o'clock in the morning when they need to be sleeping. An adolescent who can't hear their alarm clock go off for school in the morning has this unique ability to hear the intrusive ding on their phone, while in a dead sleep, from someone who is sending them a message. This brings us to our last reason we preach the importance of shutting devices down at night: what is behind the intrusive "ding?"

Usually, it's drama created by peers who are engaging late into the night about situations or rumors, perceived horrific outcomes that they need to prepare for in that moment, all intensified by the emotions and reactions of every teenager in the message thread. And, if your child is accessible, they will now be a part of this drama. Control what you can, which is your child's availability to the intrusive "ding."

Social Connection in a Digital Age

When it comes to raising kids in this digital age, we like to make the distinction between healthy solitude and unhealthy isolation. We each need some downtime to recuperate, and it is okay to just want the sacred space of one's bedroom for a short period of time. However, many of the children in the families we support can lean too heavily toward the need for this downtime, which becomes unhealthy isolation.

Frequently, they try to meet the need for healthy solitude while they are plugged-in while in their bedrooms, potentially not getting any actual seclusion. Often their argument for this type of downtime is because they are being social when interacting with friends through gaming. It is good to support this kind of downtime, within limits, and to clarify that part of the expectation is that their downtime and their social time needs to include time off screens.

To do this, they will need you to implement and monitor time limits to help them be successful. If your child is one who historically acts out of frustration when time limits are set or says, "I'm 16 and you should let me manage it on my own," then you need to ensure consistency with follow-through so they can adapt to your expectations. To the acting-out child, we might suggest offering the opportunity to course correct by saying, "I am going to come back in five minutes and if you are not able to unplug without a fight, then you are suggesting you are not ready for this kind of privilege yet." To the 16-year-old who wants to manage it for themselves, this is a great opportunity for the Book of Asks. "Ok, so you would like to be able to manage it more yourself. For now, the answer is 'no,' but we will talk about what we would need to see from you to support that and what responsibilities might need to increase for you to increase your privileges."

If you have a neurodiverse child who struggles socially, work with their treatment team to uncover activities with others that are more manageable for their tolerance. You do not want to push them so far out of their comfort zone that it causes panic, but you also don't want to allow them to stay too anchored to the comfort zone that they are isolating and not practicing competence-building skills. Work with your child and their therapist to determine the line between isolation and solitude and create parameters that support a healthy balance.

Different Rules for Different Kids

Depending on the age and maturity of your children, it is appropriate to have different rules. Actually, having different rules for different children is a necessity in parenting and an area that all kids use to scream out the injustices in the family, arguing about who gets what and why that entitles them to get it too. One counterargument to this common "unfairness" that you will be accused of is found in the cycle of responsibility and privilege. The more responsibility one shows, the more privilege one gets. Just as the more privileges we have, the more responsibilities we take on. It's just a basic life lesson that is applied to all of us and is so simple in its teaching that it allows you as the parent to just implement the teaching with each individual child.

You may have one child who can stay on top of expectations, who naturally lives a more balanced life and who does not argue when you take devices out of their room before bed. That child can have more privileges with screens because of the responsibility they demonstrate. If you have a child that is more easily distracted, prefers to isolate on devices than do much else and struggles with allowing you to parent them around their device use, then you will need to play a more active role by decreasing the freedom and privileges in order to encourage increased responsibility.

 **Nugget of Knowledge:** Increase your child's responsibility, decrease their entitlement.

In preparation to implement different rules, specifically with your child who is returning home, recognizing the old patterns and setting up a plan to minimize the reintroduction of them is important. Additionally, as you take the time to support your child's transition home from treatment, take into consideration what that support needs to look like from you as their parent to help increase their success. Going from a highly structured setting that created a healthy rhythm for him, back into the home with more temptations will be difficult. No matter how much desire he has, or you have for him, to reconnect with peers and life, your limitations and container in the home will help him sustain that much relied upon healthy rhythm even while his siblings(s) may have different ones.

Substance Use

Our experience in transition support is that some adolescents and young adults coming out of treatment want to convince themselves and their parents that they can be a casual user and still be successful. This is hard to digest and something difficult for parents to hear, especially after the commitments, sacrifices, and investments everyone has made in treatment. It's a high-risk behavior that can cause intense feelings and for some parents even trigger post-traumatic stress.

Our guidance in working with parents who find themselves on the receiving end of conversations like this is to acknowledge these intense emotions while staying grounded in your expectations. Hold on to your knowledge about what is in your control and what is not. Be clear in your boundaries that you are not supporting any attempts at casual drug use and that you will have a response if they choose to take this risk. Remind yourself that it's your child who will need to adjust to your boundary and not you who must adjust to their desire.

In a world where marijuana is legal for recreational use in many states, parents are faced with this argument from their children. We often remind parents that alcohol is also legal and ask parents what their stance has been around use of alcohol, along with asking parents to examine their own substance use. In the treatment world, when substance abuse is a pattern or a high risk for a child, we focus on the importance of helping the child's brain develop while sober for as long as possible, giving their brains the best chance to fully develop. At home, we have less control, and this is a high-risk area that deserves emotional currency and a clear value set that drives parents forward.

When addressing what we have control over, which often is the power of the purse, it is important to note that a substance using child can use any cash they have access to for purchasing their drug of choice, especially if the parents are financially covering other wants and needs, allowing the child the freedom to spend money on what they want. If you do not want your child's substance use to be a line item in your budget, consider their financial responsibilities along with your financial support of unnecessary items. We encourage parents to consistently make the distinction between paying for "life" (needs) and "lifestyle" (wants) as you consider what you are offering and providing.

We have found that the parents we work with are further successful with increasing what they will support financially and privileges they offer when their child is consistently invested in not using as well as invested in proving their abstinence. We also encourage parents to consider the risks they are taking by allowing the use of a car for a substance-using child when their use has been a part of their treatment focus. Implementing the concepts of allowing for time to see what healthy rhythms your child is willing to establish and what responsibility they are willing to take on, will then allow you to consider more privileges while acknowledging this particular privilege comes with a great responsibility.

 **Nugget of Knowledge:** As you consider the H.O.M.E. model and ask what you might need to **master** in relation to substance use, we tend to encourage parents to **master** their own healthy coping skills as well as their own moderation or sobriety.

Consequences

Consequences are one of the most challenging areas for the parents we work with, and a slew of questions are consistent. *How do we decide on consequences? Con-*

sequences have never seemed to work with our child, so what do we do? We never can come up with the consequences that match the behavior. In general, consequences are draining, difficult to identify, and so hard to implement that when doing so, parents can feel as if they are being punished more than their child. All true, we agree, and it's part of parenting, maybe even seen as the most undesirable part of the job.

As we look at why we use consequences, more often than not, it's used as a form of leverage to increase the likelihood of the behavioral change we want to see our child have. When we have expectations of our children and they don't respond accordingly to those expectations, we use consequences to redirect them, with the intention to create incentive for change. It all sounds so easy and effective when we describe it. Yet, we know it's not.

Implementation is always the hardest part and a way to ease the difficulty is to remember that "to discipline is to teach," and when you discipline with a consequence, it is helpful to ask yourself, "what is it that I am attempting to teach my child?" Sometimes it's to teach the importance of reflecting on choices, sometimes it's to teach how to redirect behaviors. Often, it's to teach that the choices we make come with a response and sometimes that response has a natural, undesirable consequence.

However, the difficulty in allowing for natural con-sequences comes from the fact that children don't have lives that include a lot of opportunity for natural consequences, which can seem so inherent in the lives of adults. We are then left to use contrived consequences to help us teach them the importance of action and response, that choices matter, and all choices will have an outcome. While it's sometimes all we have, it is undesirable as most adults don't live in a contrived world, so it makes implementing anything contrived even more difficult.

In our experience, parents often lean too much on the approach that a "punishment must match the crime" when identifying consequences. While this approach at times can work, especially when it appears to offer the feel of a natural consequence, it often is one of the leading causes of what drains a parent. Parents can't be expected to have a consequence to match every behavior. And even if you could, it would move you away from focusing on what it is you're trying to teach your child and keep you stuck in punishment mode.

We encourage parents to come up with a handful – a basketful, if you will – of consequences that each parent can not only support, but be comfortable and able to implement on their own. The easiest way to identify the contrived consequences for your basket is to identify your leverages. Basically, what is it that is important to your child? What do they care about? What will they miss if they don't have it?

The encouragement behind this basketful approach also allows you to assess your own bandwidth when it comes to having to execute a consequence. A parent's lack of energy or mental capacity while attempting to implement a consequence may be the number one reason for a parent's perceived failure at being successful with consequences. If you have a basket full of consequences and you know all of them will "pack a punch" because your child cares about them or will miss them if they don't have them, then it really doesn't matter which one you pick, as they all give you the leverage you are looking for to create a behavioral change. What *does* matter is whether the one you pick is the one you have the bandwidth to execute, creating chances of greater success.

Even when you find the one consequence that you do have the energy to implement and even if it's one of your most successful options, it still can be exhausting, especially with a child who has no desire to make it easy for you. So, consider this Nugget of Knowledge, "simply not letting things go unnoticed can be consequence enough." Let's celebrate that parenting concept!

You can make it clear that you are not naïve to what is going on and you can make an "I hope" statement without implementing a consequence. The "I hope" statement should be held in as high regard as the "I feel" statement. Really, it's a brilliant sentence starter, giving you, the parent, the opportunity to teach or even tell your child what you would like them to hear or consider without the ineffective, long, drawn out parent lecture.

This approach of not letting the behavior, the dirty look, the passive aggressive comment go unnoticed and using the "I hope" statement, gives a nudge and offers the opportunity for your child to course correct.

"I saw that you were on your phone later than we agreed last night and I hope that you can create a system for yourself that will help you get off screens on time."

Or,

"I saw the dirty look you gave me when you left the kitchen this morning after I said 'no' to what you wanted and I hope next time you can find a different and kinder way to communicate your feelings with me."

This can be a comment made in passing and does not need to be a sit-down conversation – a parenting on-the-fly moment. This approach is especially useful when you are seeing incidents (but not patterns) and gives the chance to respond in kind without making it a bigger deal than it is.

 **Nugget of Knowledge:** Simply not letting things go unnoticed can be consequence enough.

Reasonable Time & Allowing for Recovery

Hopelessness that the hardship won't end, for a child who gets a consequence, and ineffectual consequences can occur when parents tend to react emotionally to their child's behavior.

"I reacted with the nuclear option again and told her she was grounded for the month. She and I both know I won't follow through with it, so how do I come back from this?"

The first step, before the nuclear option, is to buy yourself time to acknowledge and address the emotions you are experiencing so that you are not reactive to them. Reminding yourself that you do not have to give a consequence right in the moment and waiting does not mean that you are letting your child get away with something. Waiting actually means you are committing to taking time to decide how you want to respond. This offers you the time to gather data, collect puzzle pieces, and examine how your child is doing in other areas of her life in addition to the situation that is inviting you to consider a consequence. You can take the time to discuss with your co-parent if you have one as well, so that you can determine a middle-ground option and make a wise-minded decision together.

The second step is to be aware of what you are saying when it comes to the length of time that you are committing to the consequence taking place. For however long you state the consequence will be in place, what you are really saying is, "this is how long I am committing to holding you accountable with this particular consequence." When you throw out a length of time that everyone in the room knows you will not be able to or want to follow through with, you again put yourself in a position to be seen as untrustworthy as a parent; a parent who just threatens and doesn't stand by their word.

We created an approach that we call the 24-72-hour rule with establishing consequences. The rule is simply this: don't put a consequence in place for any length of time less than 24 hours or more than 72 hours. By establishing this rule, you offer your child an opportunity to reflect, recover and try again. In addition to using discipline to teach behavioral modification, it's important to also teach recovery; how one recovers from a conflict or from making a poor decision. To do this, we can capitalize on another skill set that your child gained from their time is treatment which is to reflect on their thoughts, experiences, feelings, and decisions.

When you use a more manageable length of time when implementing a consequence, you are giving your child the opportunity to reflect on their decisions while meeting their consequence. If the time period is too short (less than 24 hours), there is not enough time to truly feel the impact of the consequence and to reflect on the decisions. If the time period is too long (over 72 hours) then the opportunity for reflection is lost because other emotions like hopelessness, frustration, blame can take over simply because it's too long of a period for consistent reflection.

The 24-72-hour time period also gives a true opportunity for recovery, a chance to use the information from their time in reflection to implement a "try again" attitude, hopefully resulting in a different decision the next time they are in a similar situation. This approach also allows you as the parent to utilize the "I hope" statement to give direction to what you hope they will reflect on.

"Matt, I am taking your phone away for the next 48 hours because of how disrespectful you were towards me. My hope is that during that time you will think about how you can communicate your frustrations with me in a more respectful way even when you are mad or don't like what I have said or done." In this example, the goal then would be for Matt to get his phone back after 48 hours, during which time he hopefully will have considered different ways to communicate next time he is frustrated with his parents. This approach offers the opportunity for Matt, in this case, to be held accountable to a behavior with a consequence that is doable for his parents to implement, giving him the opportunity to reflect and recover so he can try again next time.

We find this rule to be ideal for the co-parenting team as well. It offers a commitment to fall in line with and a way to minimize the unhealthy compensation that can happen especially for co-parenting teams when there is one parent who may administer consequences too much or too harshly in the length of time and one who may not use consequences enough. The approach looks like this: a co-parenting team makes a commitment that when independently putting a consequence in place, they will stick to the 24-72-hour rule. If one parent gives a consequence for 24 hours and the other parent says they would have given the consequence for at least 48 hours, that can be a conversation to be had but not a decision to change because the parent fell in line with the commitment the co-parenting team had.

Again, as in any tool we teach, there is room for modification based on the situation a parent is navigating. Often, parents will ask if it always has to be at least 24 hours and the answer is 'no,' but be cautious, because when there is minimal time for reflection, kids are just relying on their ability to perform to get back to what they desire to be doing. On the flip side, parents will ask if there are situations where 72 hours is not long enough, and the answer is 'absolutely.' The guidance is, don't make that decision unilaterally, only make that decision when the co-parenting team comes together to decide that it's necessary for a longer-term consequence to achieve the teachable outcome.

There are situations that benefit from a different response and some of these situations you can also predict and prepare for. For example, it is often recommended that substance use is a "non-negotiable" behavior with a zero-tolerance policy. It's crucial for you to really understand if this approach is a fit for you by talking about what it truly means to you and how you will implement it. When we are asked about consequences for positive drug tests, in addition to considering the financial relationship, we encourage parents to first look at all of the puzzle pieces to determine what sort of consequences makes sense.

A child who is doing reasonably well in five out of six areas in life and who tested positive for the first time may get a different response than a child who is struggling in multiple areas and has used more than once. While you do not want to give permission to use as long as "things are going okay" you still might have a different response such as, "this still crosses a boundary for us, though we see how hard you are working in other areas. If you test positive again or start to struggle more, our response will be tougher but for now we are going to limit some of the privileges you have been given including the use of the car until you test negative."

This approach offers you the opportunity to respond vs. react because you predicted and prepared and you actively followed through with your parenting commitment to drug test. It offered you the chance to show that you will not let behaviors go unnoticed, you will intervene in your child's choices by implementing a consequence to discourage the behavior and you're giving a chance for recovery: an opportunity for them to try again.

Encourage Competency

In addition to moving past the need to punish and into the value of teaching, think about consequences as a way to encourage competency.

"Alesha spent days brushing me off when I was asking her to help with things around the house and she kept prioritizing whatever she was doing on the phone over any help around the house. So, following your guidance, I took away devices from her for three days and told her that if, during those three days, I witnessed her helping out when asked, even if she wasn't happy about it, and showing that she could prioritize some needs over wants, then she could get the devices back. If she continued to struggle with those things, then I would keep the phone until she showed some healthy rhythm with responding to requests before I gave her back the thing that distracted her from it. She showed her willingness and competency for three days and got the phone back with the agreement that, if it becomes a struggle again then she will lose devices and we will try another reset. I have not had to take the phone since then and it has been three weeks!"

This is a great example of a parent getting clear with expectations and acknowledging the obstacles, which include the normalcy of device distraction. Additionally, identifying what her child needs in order for her, the parent, to feel assured that giving the device back with the opportunity to try again will most likely bring success when similar experiences present themselves. Many parents need to go through practices like this several times, showing their children that they will truly follow through with what they say, before their children are able to change their behavior. In this model, you can value the competencies as much as you value the punishment and give yourself and your child a clear path to the other side, which can stave off hopelessness.

When parents focus on encouraging competency, it's a natural reminder that some situations need a conversation, which can require collaboration from your child. This is a time when you can use an effective parenting tool: asking your child to share two pros and two cons to whatever decision they made, increasing the opportunity and practice of critical thinking. When enacting such a tool, it is important to continue to maintain realistic expectations.

"We asked Allie today about the pros and cons of changing from private school to public school and at first, she said there were no cons. She said that the pros were that she was more likely to have friends at a bigger school, that she would not have to wear a uniform and that the classes would be easier."

Let us tell you two things about this example to help build the foundation of your own critical thinking:

1) Typically, when a child says there are no cons or that they don't know the answer to the question the parent is asking, parents are quick to jump in and give the answers they "should have" come up with. Parents need to keep quiet and instead say, "well, I am happy to share some of my thoughts but first, and if you want us to consider what you are asking for, we need to see that you can look at it from both sides." Helping your child to develop critical thinking skills can be more important than the decision they ultimately land on.

2) Notice that the answers are what you might consider to be immature. They are not focused on how the decision will contribute to a brighter future, but they are focused on friends, clothing, and ease of life. This is appropriate, depending on the age, capability, and developmental skills of your child. And this is why you do not give them control over all their decisions. The process of asking for pros and cons is not to get them to consider things as an adult would, it is just to push for flexible thinking, even if the answers seem subpar to you. In most big situations, you are still in charge, but it can be good to use them as opportunities to develop critical thinking.

You can also ask your child to step into your shoes and share with you what he thinks your concerns are about the situation, rather than you being the one to express concerns to him. This can change the power dynamic and the tone of the conversation. You don't need to interrupt or add to what he is saying if he does well enough. Keep in mind your realistic expectations with how you define "well enough", which doesn't mean articulating as a high-functioning adult, but rather giving you an irritated speech from a child who is getting in trouble and just wants out of the conversation. You can still identify the potential consequence if the line is crossed again, and some parents do well with asking their child what they see as an appropriate consequence.

Understand, however, that some children, whose emotions are heightened and critical thinking skills are limited, might not come up with much in the moment and you do not want their hesitancy to lead to additional conflict. If they cannot come up with ideas, you can let them know that if they ever do think of one that they can share it, otherwise you will be in charge of creating the consequences.

Above all, when you are considering consequences, remember that there is no way you are going to be able to prepare for everything that might be coming. If you have a wise-minded habit where you slow down, ask yourself a few essential questions, and you are willing to consider all of your options to help you decide how to respond, then you don't need a specific plan for managing each situation. By removing the pressure from yourself to have an immediate response or to execute a consequence in the moment while giving yourself permission to reserve the right to parent in this way, it will empower you and give you the strength you need in those difficult times.

Chapter 13

Supporting Siblings Through the Transition Home

As you welcome your child home from treatment, there are a few predictable situations with siblings to be prepared for.

We find that, regardless of the age of siblings at home, they are often asked to be the bigger people as their sibling transitions home. In ways, often reminiscent of the past, siblings are encouraged to walk on eggshells. In this situation, as a way to express understanding and that this transition will be hard for the child who has been away. The reality is of course that the transition can be tough for everyone in the family. While it makes sense that you want the siblings to try to be understanding, you also want them to know that you are understanding that they are also faced with challenges. Some of them were afraid of the sibling who went to treatment and will be unsure what to trust as they come back into the home. Some siblings will have enjoyed being the only child for a while and they will be back to vying for attention, potentially in unhealthy ways.

So, when challenges between siblings arise, instead of just asking for compassion toward the child who has just come home, make sure that you are **enacting** compassion over the situation for the sibling as well. And, make sure that you leave some space for siblings to work things out on their own. Perhaps you can offer a passing comment that empowers them while letting them know that you are there if needed. For example, "I see you two getting into it and believe you can work it out. Let me know if you get stuck and need my support." Certainly, if the scene is unsafe, intervene but give equal compassion to the child seen as the perpetrator as you do to the perceived victim.

On the coattails of the aforementioned is being aware of who is getting the air in the room. Prior to treatment, there was typically a lot of air in the room taken by the child who was struggling the most. While they were in treatment, that child continued to take up airtime as parents engaged in phone calls, letter writing, concern over the child's progress and time consuming moments spent on deciding on the steps after treatment.

Now, as they transition home, the air that the siblings were able to muster will again be shared. When those challenges arise, make sure that you offer time to the siblings to share their perspective, perhaps also asking them what they wish their sibling understood about them, rather than asking the sibling to just focus on stepping into the shoes of the child who has just returned.

Some siblings will be delighted in the return of their partner in crime or BFF. And the siblings at home might have more relaxed screen rules, which can lead the child who has just returned home to lean on their siblings to use their social media. Make sure your expectations are clear and you avoid guilting a supportive sibling who may struggle and give in to the sibling who is home from treatment. Don't say, "If you give her money, or let her use your technology she could end up back in treatment." Do say, "We are trying to help her make good decisions and hope you can support that in times when you feel pressured. Feel free to let us know if you get stuck with something or feel trapped into doing something you don't want."

Siblings need the space to be siblings again and sometimes what is a developmentally appropriate sibling situation can feel scary for parents who have the pain of the recent past impacting the lenses through which they see it. While you might want to protect them from each other so that the tone of the sibling relationships does not end up where it used to be, make sure that a situation needs your intervening before you dive in. Allow for the possibility that new skills exist and allow the time for them to rise to the surface. This is also the time to consider if any outside support is needed in the sibling relationship to help repair and strengthen it.

Oftentimes seeking out a family therapist who is willing to support siblings as one version of family therapy is ideal. You most likely will not have children doing cartwheels over this idea and as the parent committed to the whole system changing, can forcefully encourage it for a handful of sessions and then see what continues to be needed.

Chapter 14

Celebration

Prior to your journey with your child through the treatment process, you were on high alert, aware of risky behaviors, inundated with concerning moments, and often in crisis mode. As a result, and because you don't have experiences at home with your child showing up with their newfound behaviors, it might be challenging to shift your focus. You will be tempted to notice and maybe even be hyperalert to the old behaviors as you question whether you have made the right decision to support your child at home. To change your internal tone and the tone of the home, it is vital that you put an equal amount of effort into noticing the strength moments. You don't need to throw a party when your child brushes their teeth without reminders but make sure to offer authentic validation when you witness character traits that could benefit from reinforcement.

Validating character traits takes the binary "good" or "bad" and encourages a bit more effort by noticing when someone is thoughtful, or hard working or patient. Your job is to have it in your awareness when the strength moments happen as an antidote to the tendency to wait for the struggle moments and just keep score of those. At times, we have parents who will just focus on the not so great behavior they have seen through the week. We often suggest to these parents who need to keep a list, that they consider including these topics:

- A list of the strength moments they validated through the week or that they witnessed, even if they did not validate it.
- A list of their strengths and struggles through the week. This shifts the focus from keeping score of your child's behaviors and invites insight into yourself as well. When you follow through with this, you can be more intentional with the time you spend enticing and celebrating their strengths.

The concept of puzzle pieces plays a role here as well; remember, the idea is to allow time to pass before you place meaning on a situation. When it seems like something hasn't gone well, before you determine that it is a major struggle that requires intervening or before you assume that the situation suggests that your child is not doing well, see what happens over a few days. If you allow for more of the pieces to come together over a period of time, you might find that you have a longer list of strengths than you do of struggles and you need to put an equal amount of time celebrating, whether to yourself or out loud, the moments that go well.

Celebrate your children and yourselves. Take notice and acknowledge the moments where more times than not your child followed your expectation or when he offered to help out without being asked or responded to a request without the teenage tone that gets under your skin. Whatever it is, notice and celebrate, even if it's just internal. External celebrations like getting ice cream are just as useful, especially when the whole family gets to celebrate everyone's effort in the transition.

Opportunities for spontaneous "we are rocking it this week" celebrations as a family can go a long way, too. And celebrate yourself. Notice your strength moments, notice times when you misstep and recover, notice when you prioritize your own healthy rhythm, when you ask for help, when you buy time, when you are curious, and when you respond rather than react. Celebrate how far you have come and celebrate the changes in the tone of the home that you are **enacting.**

Remember. Reflect. Revisit.

- The power is in your parenting, not in the piece of paper.
- Find your people and help your child find theirs.
- Check with your treatment team to ensure that your expectations are developmentally appropriate for your child's strengths and struggles; make sure expectations of yourself are also reasonable.
- Keep a let's keep trying attitude and **own** your boundaries, expectations and your tone.
- Make time to review your home agreements, assess and rework as necessary with a thoughtful process rather than impulsive changes driven by demands from your child.
- Consistency is key; be consistent, not rigid.
- Throw electronics out the window… or reintroduce them thoughtfully while prioritizing sleep and balanced living.
- Be radically honest about your own substances use as you shape the guardrails to encourage your child's sobriety.

- Use consequences to teach, not to punish.
- Make consequences matter with the 24/72 hour rule.
- Value competency and offer clarity about what competency looks like in a specific situation and how you will honor it if witnessed… spontaneous rewards go a long way.
- Celebrate how far you have come and celebrate the changes in the tone of the home that you are **enacting.**

Chapter 15

The End... or the Beginning

The H.O.M.E. model invites you to address this journey with your family through identifying where you land on the continuum of **hone, own, master, enact**. The goal is to empower you, parents, to engage in and sustain your personal growth through situational self-assessment. From the moment you opened this book, and potentially the beginning of your child's time in treatment, you accepted the invitation to delve past the surface to understand the norms that had taken over your home, to take a sacred pause to better understand yourself, and you have proactively moved forward with shaping a new tone and rhythm with which to welcome your child home.

There is so much you need to be truly ready for and there is not enough time in the world to get there, because the truth is that, at some point, you and your child are as ready as you can be, and you just need to try. However, this is not permission to let things go with an "it is what it is" mentality. By having a basic understanding of our guiding principles, you can affect the lens through which you view what is ahead, through which you view the world around you now.

Walking alongside your child in treatment while continuing to show up for yourself and your family at home, you learn to look in the mirror with the intention of understanding and without judgment, guilt, and shame. With dedication and commitment to this process and with acknowledgment that it does not end with wilderness therapy or even with longer term residential treatment, you can **own** the steps you want to take and offer opportunities within which your children make choices, as you also aim to let go of control.

The bad news is, you are going to screw up. The good news is, not everything is your fault, you will also get things right, and no one is expecting perfection. All of which are important to keep in mind as you anticipate how your family will manage through this transition. Just like you want your kids to work hard to thrive at home, we want you to work hard as well, while embodying a gentle tone with yourselves and each other. The difficulties you could face can stir up recent traumas as well as older ones and ensuring you have your own support through this process is essential. Whether that is through a personal therapist, a coach, a solid group of friends, or a healthy rhythm that replenishes you and helps you to regulate yourself, find your safety net.

This book is meant to come alongside you through this process and there might be times when it makes sense to go back through and revisit sections. There might come a time when you want a refresher on the guiding principles or a reminder on standing strong and **owning** your commitments that are crucial reminders to help you not fall back into old patterns... spend some time again in Part 1. Perhaps there will be a moment in the future when you become aware that you are disconnected from yourself or that you have lost your rhythm... take a moment in the sacred pause and find some words of wisdom that can help. Or maybe as you remember that the power is in the parenting and not the piece of paper, you want to reexamine your role in shaping your home and tap back into to **mastery** in Part 3 that can help you stake claim again in what you have control over.

As this book comes to an end, and perhaps as your child's time in treatment comes to an end, keep in mind that this is a new beginning. The journey doesn't end here, and you are equipped with new awareness and skills to bring with you as you take your first next steps together and H.O.M.E. is here to help along the way.

Following Your Path Journals

H.O.M.E. Publishing's Hilary Moses and Jen Murphy are proud to offer their Following Your Path journals. These journals, one for adolescents and young adults and the other for parents, were inspired by Jen and Hilary's lessons from working with clients, first as wilderness therapists and now while guiding families through major transitions.

The journal exercises have been curated specifically for families transitioning their child back home from wilderness therapy and other extended treatment programs. The journals encourage engagement in the newfound skills honed in treatment and help with navigating the challenging situations that will arise.

Owning your role in this process, engaging in these journals daily, and responding to the prompts within provides helpful insight and increases the self-awareness necessary to find the strength and the support needed to thrive. The Following Your Path journals are intended to support a young person and a parent as soon as transition planning is initiated and are an invaluable resource when used at the very beginning of the transition home.

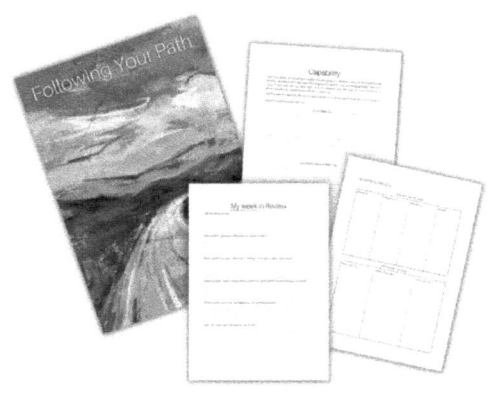

Order your journal at
www.solutionsparentingsupport.com/journal

References

Abrams, J. and Zweig, C. (1991) *Meeting the Shadow: The hidden power of the dark side of human nature.* Los Angeles: J.P. Tarcher.

Allen, S., 2018. A white paper prepared for the John Templeton Foundation by the Greater ... Available at: https://ggsc.berkeley.edu/images/uploads/GGSC-JTF_White_Paper-Awe_FINAL.pdf [Accessed September 16, 2022].

Anon, Shame definition & meaning. Merriam-Webster. Available at: https://www.merriam-webster.com/dictionary/shame [Accessed September 20, 2022].

Berg, P., The Tao of Teenagers: A Guide to Teen Health, Happiness and Empowerment ... Available at: https://www.amazon.com/Tao-Teenagers-Health-Happiness-Empowerment/dp/0692756795 [Accessed September 20, 2022].

Brown Brené, 2017. Rising Strong, New York: Spiegel & Grau.

DeAngelis, T., 2013. Therapy Gone Wild. Monitor on Psychology. Available at: https://www.apa.org/monitor/2013/09/therapy-wild [Accessed September 16, 2022].

Emerald, D., 2010. The Power of TED: The Empowerment Dynamic, Bainbridge Island, WA: Polaris Pub.

Rite of Passage (2021) *Open Sky.* Available at: https://www.openskywilderness.com/rite-of-passage/ (Accessed: November 25, 2022).

Florence, J., 2017. Emotional Currency, the Underlying Exchange. HuffPost. Available at: https://www.huffpost.com/entry/emotional-currency-the-underlying-exchange_b_5870780 [Accessed September 20, 2022].

Fritscher, L. (2021) *Recovering from the Fear of Vulnerability, Verywell Mind.* Verywell Mind. Available at: https://www.verywellmind.com/fear-of-vulnerability-2671820 (Accessed: November 5, 2022).

Gonzales, K., 2022. Why We Use The Term 'Emerging Adults'. The Imprint. Available at: https://imprintnews.org/opinion/why-we-use-the-term-emerging-adults/62667 [Accessed September 16, 2022].

Horowitz, R.C., 2011. Family Centered Parenting: Your Guide for Growing Great Families, Garden City, NY: Morgan James Publishing.

Kreisman, J.J. and Straus, H. (2021) *I Hate You, Don't Leave Me: Understanding the Borderline Personality.* New York: Perigee Books.

Lisitsa, E., 2022. The Four Horsemen: The Antidotes. The Gottman Institute. Available at: https://www.gottman.com/blog/the-four-horsemen-the-antidotes/ [Accessed September 16, 2022].

Lucariello, J., Top 20 Principles Form Psychology for Prek-12 Teaching and Learning. BOOKS FOR PSYCHOLOGY CLASS. Available at: https://booksforpsychologyclass.weebly.com/blog/june-05th-2015 [Accessed September 20, 2022].

Meltzer, R., 2007. Life Learning Plan

Milkman, K., 2022. How To Change: The Science Of Getting To Where You Want To Be, London: Vermilion.

Moses, H. and Murphy, J. What's Going Well Meeting Outline. Available at: Solutionsparentingsupport.com/home

Moses, H. and Murphy, J. Book of Asks. Available at: Solutionsparentingsupport.com/home

Munsey, C., Emerging Adults: The in-between age. Monitor on Psychology. Available at: https://www.apa.org/monitor/jun06/emerging [Accessed September 19, 2022].

Nelson, P., 2018. There's a Hole in My Sidewalk: The Romance of Self-Discovery, New York: Atria Paperbacks.

Patterson, K. *et al.* (2012) *Crucial Conversations: Tools for Talking When Stakes are High.* New York etc.: McGraw-Hill.

Payne, K.J., 2021. The Soul of Discipline: The simplicity parenting approach to warm, firm, and calm guidance--from toddlers to teens, New York: Ballantine Books.

Quintero, N., Transforming the Mindset: Psychology professor Carol S. Dweck, Phd, speaks at the United Nations. American Psychological Association. Available at: https://www.apa.org/international/pi/2015/03/transforming-mindset [Accessed September 20, 2022].

Robbins, T. (no date) *Why Meaning is Everything • Power of Reframing: Tony Robbins, tonyrobbins.com.* Available at: https://www.tonyrobbins.com/why-meaning-is-everything/ (Accessed: March 14, 2022).

Shelly Bullard, M.F.T., 2021. 4 Truths About A Sacred Relationship. mindbodygreen. Available at: https://www.mindbodygreen.com/0-25828/4-truths-about-a-sacred-relationship.html [Accessed September 16, 2022].

Siegel, D. & Rock, D., 2020. Healthy Mind Platter. Dr. Dan Siegel. Available at: https://drdansiegel.com/healthy-mind-platter/ [Accessed September 16, 2022].

Siegel, D.J. and Bryson, T.P. (2016) *The Whole-Brain Child: 12 revolutionary strategies to nurture your child's developing Mind.* Vancouver, B.C.: Langara College.

Stevens, R.T. et al., 2007. Conscious Language: The Logos of Now: The Discovery, code and upgrade to our new conscious human operating system, Asheville, NC: Mastery Systems.

Stuart, G., 2020. What are Authoritarian, Permissive, Uninvolved and Authoritative Parenting Styles? Sustaining Community. Available at: https://sustainingcommunity.wordpress.com/2015/02/04/what-are-parenting-styles/ [Accessed September 16, 2022].

Suttie, J.J., How to Listen to Pain. Greater Good. Available at: https://greatergood.berkeley.edu/article/item/how_to_listen_to_pain [Accessed September 20, 2022].

Tim Ferriss: Bestselling Author, H.G.P., 2020. The Tim Ferriss Show: #409: Brené Brown - striving versus self-acceptance, saving marriages, and more on Apple Podcasts. Apple Podcasts. Available at: https://podcasts.apple.com/us/podcast/409-bren%C3%A9-brown-striving-versus-self-acceptance-saving/id863897795?i=1000464823494 [Accessed September 16, 2022].

Weir, K. (2020) *Nurtured by Nature, Monitor on Psychology.* American Psychological Association. Available at: https://www.apa.org/monitor/2020/04/nurtured-nature (Accessed: April 8, 2022).

Find more information and additional resources visit:
www.SolutionsParentingSupport.com/home

About the Authors

Jen Murphy, M.Ed., is a highly accomplished psycho-therapist with an extensive career as a wilderness therapist and is an adjunct faculty member in the Social Sciences Department at Colorado Mountain College. In addition, she has developed and implemented two nationally recognized transition programs and is an expert in the field of providing effective parent coaching to parents as they transition their children home from wilderness and long-term treatment programs. Jen lives in Steamboat Springs, Colorado and is an imperfect parent who always enjoys executing forced family fun time with her husband and two sons as they navigate the teenage years.

Hilary Moses, MSW, LCSW, is a widely esteemed therapist who, throughout her career as a wilderness clinician and program clinical director, was among the most highly regarded and demanded in the field. Hilary is a national public speaker and presenter, has written and developed parenting and transition curricula, facilitated hundreds of workshops and family seminars and was an adjunct professor for the MSW program at Arizona State University's Watts College of Public Service and Community Solutions. As a step-parent since 2008, she is motivated by the experiences of co-parenting in a split family and believes that, with empowerment, en-couragement and diligence, parents who engage in their own work can greatly affect the tone of the home thus influencing the whole family's success. Hilary currently lives in Tucson, Arizona with her husband and two sons.

Learn more about the Solutions Parenting Support team:
www.solutionsparentingsupport.com

SOLUTIONS PARENTING SUPPORT